C000299750

ed by AA Publishing
mobile Association Developments
2004
ed 2005

ts reserved. No part of this publication
e reproduced, stored in a retrieval
in any form or by any means –
hic, photocopying, recording or
se – unless the written permission of
lishers has been obtained
and.

ed by AA Publishing (a trading name
mobile Association Developments
, whose registered office is
vood East, Apollo Rise, Farnborough,
hire, GU14 0JW; registered number
35)

Ordnance This product includes
Survey* mapping data licensed
rdnance Survey® with the permission
Controller of Her Majesty's Stationery

vn copyright 2005. All rights reserved.
number 399221

ISBN-10: 0-7495-4060-5
ISBN-13: 978-0-7495-4060-9

A02700

A CIP catalogue record for this book is
available from the British Library.

The contents of this book are believed
correct at the time of printing. Nevertheless,
the publishers cannot be held responsible
for any errors or omissions or for changes in
the details given in this book or for the
consequences of any reliance on the
information it provides. We have tried to
ensure accuracy, but things do change and
we would be grateful if readers would advise
us of any inaccuracies they encounter. This
does not affect your statutory rights.

Please write to:
AA Publishing, FH16, Fanum House,
Basing View, Basingstoke RG21 4EA

We have taken all reasonable steps to
ensure that these walks are safe and
achievable by walkers with a realistic level
of fitness. However, all outdoor activities
involve a degree of risk and the publishers
accept no responsibility for any injuries
caused to readers whilst following these
walks. For more advice on using this book
see page 10 and walking safely see page
112. The mileage range shown on the front
cover is for guidance only – some walks may
exceed or be less than these distances.

These routes appear in the *AA Local Walks*
series and *1001 Walks in Britain*.

Visit AA Publishing at ***www.theAA.com/
bookshop***

Colour reproduction by:
Keene Group, Andover
Printed and bound by:
Leo Paper, China

Acknowledgements

Researched and written by Des Hannigan,
Sue Viccars, Ronald Turnbull, David
Hancock and Ann F Stonehouse

Picture credits

All images are held in the Automobile
Association's own photo library (AA World
Travel Library) and were taken by the
following photographers:
Front cover ; 3 P Baker; 5 A Lawson;
6/7 R Moss; 8 R Moss; 9tc R Moss;
9tr P Kenward; 9br H Williams;
10tl P Baker; 10tc R Moss.

*Opposite: Wheal Coates engine house
stands by the coastal path in Cornwall*

The **AA** 100 Walks in
Southwest England

Prod
© Au
Limit
Repr

All rig
may
syste
electr
other
the p
befor

Publi
of Au
Limit
Sout
Ham
1878

Contents

Page 6: The ruined Chapel of
St Michael stands atop Barrow Mump
in Somerset

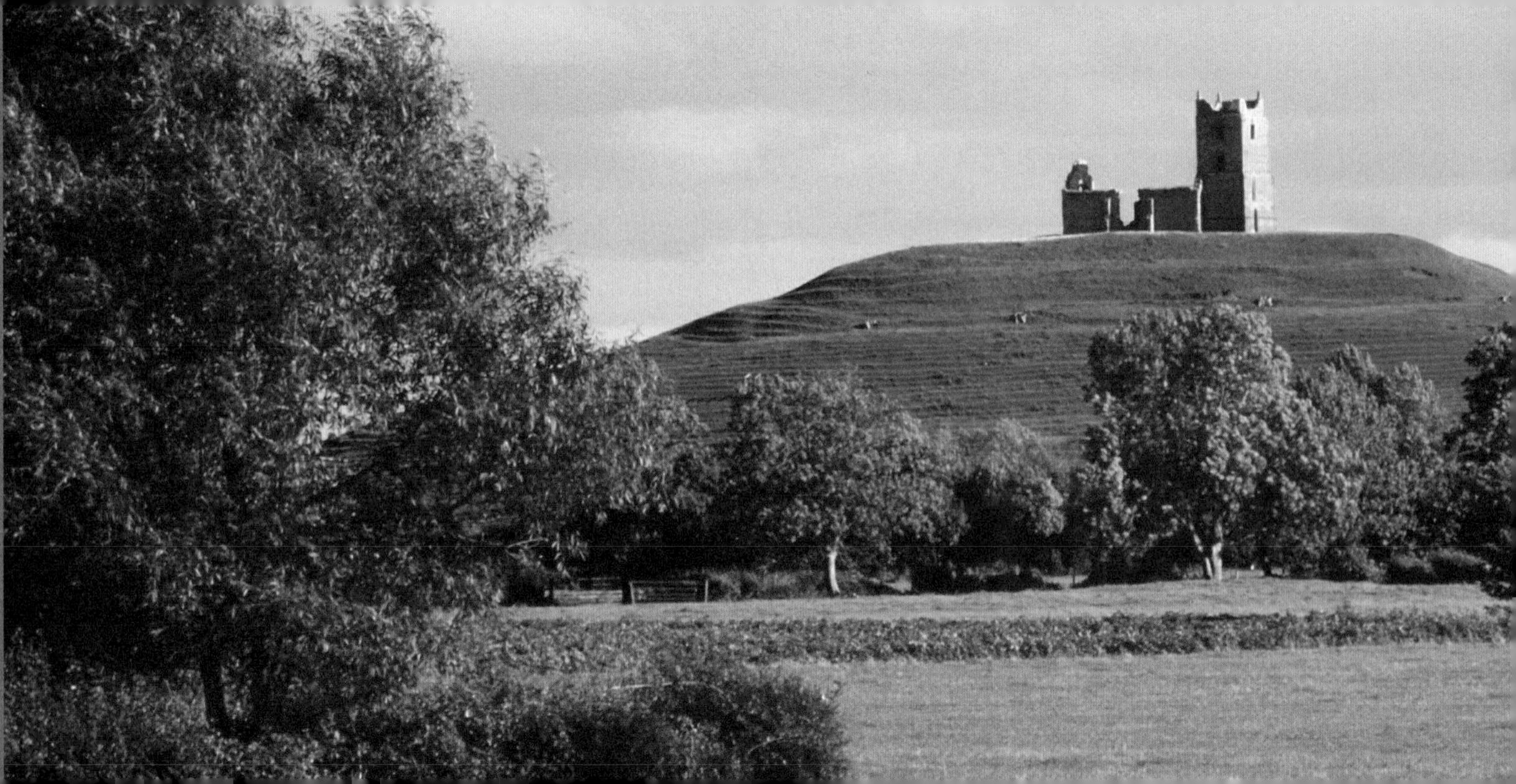

Southwest England

The southwest is defined by its coastline, its villages and its country towns rather than by great cities or industrial conurbations. Even the metropolitan centres reflect the culture of rural and maritime England.

Southwest England

Surrounded by the South West Coast Path National Trail, the maritime influence is great here, but less than a third of the walks go anywhere near to the sea. The rest are in the downland and valleys of Dorset and Wiltshire, in pastoral farmland, picturesque villages, on the moors of Somerset and Devon or on the wetlands of the Levels.

The southwest has two national parks: wild Dartmoor and the cliffs and heaths of Exmoor. Protected Areas of Outstanding Natural Beauty encompass large stretches of the Cornish coast and Bodmin Moor, parts of Devon and Dorset, the Quantock Hills in Somerset and the North Wessex Downs in Wiltshire. There are also lengths of Heritage Coast with dramatic landscapes and a rich history.
Further inland, the rural landscapes include Dorset, Wiltshire and Somerset.

Tiny villages dot the peaceful tidal creeks on the Helford Estuary

The Cornish Coast

Of the southwest coastline, the Cornish coast is probably the best-known section. In the north of the county, Morwenstow is associated with the Reverend R S Hawker, an eccentric vicar from Victoria's reign, while Crackington Haven draws students from all over the world to study the swirls and folds in its metamorphic rocks. Superlatives can be used to describe nearly every step of coastal path, and the walks explore not just idyllic rocky inlets, such as those at Prussia Cove, but also the subtropical backwaters of the Helford River and the defence systems that have guarded the Fal and Plymouth Sound for centuries. The coast, from Minehead in

Somerset to Studland in Dorset, is circumnavigated by the South West Coast Path, Britain's longest National Trail, which we have incorporated into circular walks.

You'll need a head for heights if you are to make your way comfortably along the clifftops above St Agnes Head or the Dodman. As you thread your way along old coastguard paths you will wonder that anyone scratched a living out of these inhospitable climes. But the ancient fields bear witness to many centuries of occupation, and when the industrial revolution brought new steam engines, the tin mines too were able to eke out an existence here.

The Devon Coast

Devon's coastal front is split in two. To the south, you'll find a continuation of the Cornish themes, though as the Dart, the Erme, the Avon, the Yealm and the Kingsbridge Estuary bite into the farmland of the South Hams, you'll find you're walking through an

intriguing landscape of creeks and charming villages. The ferryfolk will become your friends if you are trying to join up the sections of the coastal path here. And at Bigbury-on-Sea you'll find

they drive the most peculiar craft to get you to the offshore oasis of Burgh Island. There are no such problems awaiting you on the north Devon coast. If you negotiate the lanes to Clovelly in high season, you may rue its many charms, but venture from there on foot and you will soon leave the crowds behind.

Somerset, Dorset and Wiltshire

In Somerset you'll discover wooded coombs linking the uplands with the sea below. At East Quantoxhead is the final piece of coastal scenery you will encounter in the northern part of the region. Dorset puts its own spin

on the theme of up and down coastal paths. The highest up is on Golden Cap, sitting proudly above 627ft (191m) of fragile sandstone cliff. Like many walks here, though, you must get there from sea level – at Seatown in this case. In Purbeck, perhaps one of the loveliest parts of Dorset, a walk at Studland will give you gentle sea-level rambling as far as Bournemouth and Hengistbury Head.

Inland, Wiltshire is littered with ancient remains, but nothing compares with the ritual landscape of Avebury, where the purpose of the earthworks and alignments of stones continue to remain a mystery.

Left: Crackington Haven, Cornwall
Above: The River Stour in Dorset
Below: The South West Coast Path

Above: Cerne Abbas Giant, Dorset
Right: The Cheesewring, Bodmin Moor

Peculiar Shapes and Mysterious Lumps

The giant man at Cerne Abbas is certainly the rudest monument you'll encounter on these walks, and you will be able to make a study of pre-Roman fortifications. Badbury Rings and Cadbury Castle are perhaps the most extensive, the promontory forts of West Cornwall the most dramatic,

and Burrow Mump, above the Somerset Levels, the most singular.

Moorland Wilderness

The remains of settlements on Dartmoor and Exmoor can be traced back over 4,000 years to the Bronze Age, and these lonely moorlands escaped the rigours of agricultural change. That's not to say recent human impact has not been great on the moors of the southwest. Whether you're tracing the quarry tramways on

Bodmin Moor, crossing the great dam at Meldon Reservoir, below Dartmoor's highest peaks, or listening to the eerie rattle of the nightjar above Wimbleball Lake, reflect on the delicate balance between despoiling and enhancing our environment.

Battle Remains

The region has not been without conflict. You'll find civil war stories at Nunney, Badbury, Wardour and Winyard's Gap. At Wells, and other towns, you can learn of the Bloody Assizes, the cruel retribution meted out by James II's henchman Judge Jeffries, following the disastrous rising led by the Duke of Monmouth in 1685. The coast is littered with reminders of the Second World War. Pill boxes, like those overlooking the entrance to Plymouth Sound, would have been manned by reservists had an invasion happened. The only invasion the southwest has to deal with now is the tourists who flood in every summer to surf and sun bathe.

Using this Book

❶ Information panels
Information panels show the total distance and total amount of ascent (that is how much ascent you will accumulate throughout the walk). An indication of the gradient you will encounter is shown by the rating 0–3. Zero indicates fairly flat ground and 3 indicates undulating terrain with several very steep slopes.

❷ Minimum time
The minimum time suggested is for approximate guidance only. It assumes reasonably fit walkers and doesn't allow for stops.

❸ Start points
The start of each walk is given as a six-figure grid reference prefixed by two letters indicating which 100km square of the National Grid it refers to. You'll find more information about grid references on most Ordnance Survey maps.

00 Location Walk title

1 **2**

4½ miles (7.2km) 1hr 45min Ascent: 131ft (40m) ⚠

Paths: Cliff top, shingle beach, farm track and country lanes, 1 stile

Suggested map: OS Explorer 231 Southwold & Bungay **5**

Grid reference: TM 522818

3 **Parking:** On street near Covehithe church **6**

Country • Region

See the effects of coastal erosion on a walk along a rapidly disappearing cliff top.

1 Take tarmac lane from **St Andrew's Church** down towards sea to barrier ('Danger') and sign warning that there is no public right of way. Although this is strictly true, this is well-established and popular path stretching north towards Kessingland beach and you are likely to meet many other walkers. The warnings are serious but it is quite safe to walk here so long as you keep away from the cliff edge.

2 Walk through gap to **R** of road barrier and continue towards cliffs. Turn **L** along wide farm track with pig farm to your **L**. Path follows cliff top then descends towards beach to enter **Benacre** nature reserve. On **L** is **Benacre Broad**, once an estuary, now a marshy lagoon. The shingle beach attracts little terns in spring and summer and you should keep to the path to avoid their nesting sites.

3 Climb back on to cliffs at end of Benacre Broad. The way cuts through pine trees and bracken on constantly changing path before running alongside field and swinging **R** to descend to beach level, where you take wide grass track on your **L** across dunes.

4 At concrete track, with tower of Kessingland church in distance, turn **L** following waymarks of **Suffolk Coast and Heaths Path**. Cross stile and keep straight ahead, passing **Beach Farm** on **R**. Stay straight ahead for 1 mile (1.6km) on wide track between fields with views of Benacre church ahead.

5 Go through white gates and turn **L** on to quiet country lane. Stay on lane for ¾ mile (1.2km) as it passes between hedges with arable farmland to either side and swings **L** at entrance to **Hall Farm**.

6 When road bends **R**, turn **L** past gate with an English Nature 'No Entry' sign for cars. Stay on this permissive path as it swings **R** around meadow and continues into woodland of **Holly Grove**. Pass through another gate and turn **L** along road for ¾ mile (1.2km) back into **Covehithe**. Turn **L** at junction to return to **St Andrew's Church**.

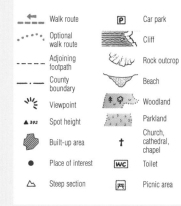

Map legend

Symbol	Name	Symbol	Name
←	Walk route	P	Car park
•••	Optional walk route	∼∼	Cliff
– – –	Adjoining footpath		Rock outcrop
–·–·–	County boundary		Beach
☀	Viewpoint	🌲	Woodland
▲ 392	Spot height		Parkland
	Built-up area	✝	Church, cathedral, chapel
●	Place of interest	WC	Toilet
△	Steep section	⛱	Picnic area

4 Abbreviations

Walk directions use these abbreviations:

L – left

L–H – left-hand

R – right

R–H – right-hand

Names which appear on signposts are given in brackets, for example ('Bantam Beach').

5 Suggested maps

Details of appropriate maps are given for each walk, and usually refer to 1:25,000 scale Ordnance Survey Explorer maps. We strongly recommend that you always take the appropriate OS map with you. Our hand-drawn maps are there to give you the route and do not show all the details or relief that you will need to navigate around the routes provided in this collection. You can purchase OS maps at all good bookshops, or by calling Stanfords on 020 7836 2260.

6 Car parking

Many of the car parks suggested are public, but occasionally you may find you have to park on the roadside or in a lay-by. Please be considerate when you leave your car, ensuring that access roads or gates are not blocked and that other vehicles can pass safely. Remember that pub car parks are private and should not be used unless you are visiting the pub or you have the landlord's permission to park there.

Morwenstow The Parson-Poet

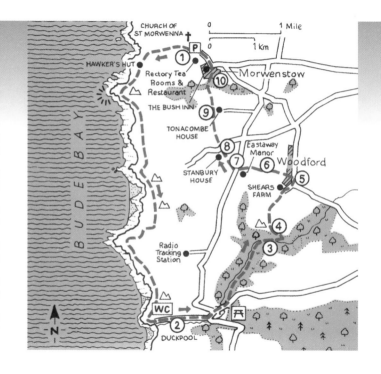

7 miles (11.3km) 4hrs **Ascent:** 1,640ft (500m) ⚠️

Paths: Generally good, but inland paths and tracks can be very muddy during wet weather

Suggested map: OS Explorer 126 Clovelly & Hartland

Grid reference: SS 206154

Parking: Morwenstow: Follow signposted road from the A39 about 2½ miles (4.4km) north of Kilkhampton. Small free car park by Morwenstow Church and Rectory Farm Tearooms

A walk in the footsteps of the eccentric Victorian poet, Reverend Robert Stephen Hawker.

❶ Follow signposted track from car park to coast path; turn **L**. Reach **Hawker's Hut** in about 100yds (91m). Continue along coast path to **Duckpool**.

❷ Reach inlet of **Duckpool**, walk up road along bottom of valley to T-junction. Turn **L**. At junction, go **R** to cross bridge beside ford. Follow lane **L** for 150yds (137m), then bear **L** on broad track through woodland.

❸ Cross stile on **L**, cross wooden footbridge, climb slope, then turn **R** and up track. Turn **L** at T-junction; keep ahead at next junction. Shortly go **R** through metal gate.

❹ Follow field track to surfaced lane at **Woodford**. Turn **L** and go downhill past **Shears Farm** then **R** and uphill to junction with road. Turn **L** past bus shelter.

❺ Turn **L** along path between cottages to kissing gate. Turn **R** then immediately **L** and follow field edge to stile on **L**. Cross stile, then next field, bearing slightly **L**, to reach hedge on opposite side.

❻ Cross 2 stiles; go straight up next field (often muddy) to hedge corner. Go alongside wall to hedged track and on to junction with surfaced lane.

❼ Go through gate opposite; turn **R** through gap. Go **L** to stile, **L** across next field to far **L-H** corner, then up to **Stanbury House**. Turn **R** to surfaced lane.

❽ Go **L** along lane then over narrow stile on **R**. Go straight across next 2 fields to stile and gate into farm lane behind **Tonacombe House**.

❾ Go **R** then bear off **L** along muddy track. Cross 2 fields; descend into wooded valley. Keep **R**, cross stream, then go **R** and up to stile (steep).

❿ Cross over fields to meadow behind **Bush Inn**. Go down **L** side of buildings, then up to road. Turn **L** for **Morwenstow Church** and car park.

Crackington Haven A Geological Phenomenon

3½ miles (5.7km) 1hr 45min **Ascent:** 270ft (82m)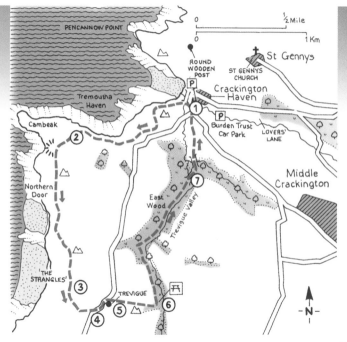

Paths: Good coastal footpath and woodland tracks. Can be very wet and muddy
Suggested map: OS Explorer 111; Bude, Boscastle & Tintagel
Grid reference: SX 145969
Parking: Crackington Haven car park. From the A39 at Wainhouse Corner, or from Boscastle on the B3263. Can be busy in summer. Burden Trust car park, along B3263 road to Wainhouse

A coastal and inland walk with spectacular sea cliff views of the North Cornish coast.

❶ From **Crackington Haven** car park entrance go **L** across bridge, then turn **R** at telephone kiosk. Follow broad track round to **L**, between signpost and old wooden seat, then go through kissing gate on to coast path.

❷ Keep **L** and follow path up sheltered valley on inland side of steep hill, then continue on cliff path (breathtaking view of folded strata and quartzite bands of **Cambeak's cliff**).

❸ Where stretch of low inland cliffs begins, just beyond signpost and shortly before 2nd signpost, go **L** along path to reach road by National Trust sign for **'The Strangles'**. Looking back from here you can see such fantastic features as **Northern Door**, promontory of harder rock pierced by its natural arch where softer shales have been eroded by sea. Track down to beach

is worthwhile despite steep return. You can view remarkable coastal features from sea level.

❹ Go **L**, walking past farm entrance to Trevigue (16th-century farmhouse), then, short distance along, turn **R** down drive by **Trevigue** sign. Bear off to **L** across grass to go through gate by signpost.

❺ Go directly down field, keeping **L** of telegraph pole, to reach stile. Continue downhill to edge of wood. Go down tree-shaded path to junction of paths in shady dell by river.

❻ Turn sharp **L** here, following signpost towards **Haven**, and continue on obvious path down wooded river valley, descending into **East Wood** (and **Trevigue valley**, much of which is now nature reserve).

❼ Cross footbridge, then turn **L** at junction with track. Cross another footbridge and continue to gate by some houses. Follow track then surfaced lane to main road, then turn **L** to return to car park.

Bodmin Moor Rocky Bounds

3 miles (4.8km) 2hrs 30min **Ascent:** 230ft (70m)

Paths: Moorland tracks and paths and disused quarry tramways
Suggested map: OS Explorer 109 Bodmin Moor
Grid reference: SX 260711
Parking: The Hurlers car park on south west side of Minions village

A walk across the wilds of Bodmin Moor.

❶ Leave car park by steps at top end beside information board (**Hurlers stone circles**). Cross grass to track. Turn **R**; follow track, passing **Hurlers** (R) and **Pipers stones** further on.

❷ At 3-way junction, by large granite block, take **R-H** track down through shallow valley bottom; climb uphill on track towards **Cheesewring Quarry**. At junction with another track, cross over and follow grassy track uphill towards quarry. At first green hillock, go **R**, then **L** to **Daniel Gumb's Cave** (18th-century stone-worker's rock house). Return to path; follow uphill alongside fenced-in rim of quarry to Cheesewring rock formation.

❸ Retrace steps towards valley bottom.

❹ Short distance from valley bottom, level with thorn trees (R) and just before fenced-off mound (L), turn **R** along path. Keep **L** of thorn trees and leaning granite block and soon find beginnings of grassy track. Follow track, keeping to R of solitary thorn tree and gorse bushes. Track becomes clearer.

❺ Track begins to strand. At leaning rock, split like whale's mouth, keep **R** along path through scrub, with rocky heights of Sharp Tor ahead. Keep to path round slope, with **Wardbrook Farm** L and **Sharptor** ahead. Reach road; turn **R** to reach open gateway.

❻ Go to **R** of fence by gateway and follow path alongside fence past 2 slim granite pillars. Join disused tramway and follow.

❼ Pass piles of broken rock and, about 30yds (27m) beyond, turn sharp **R** at wall corner. Follow green track uphill and alongside wall. Where wall ends keep on uphill to broad track.

❽ Turn **R** along track to **Cheesewring Quarry**. For main route, turn **L** and follow track to Minions village. Pass **Minions Heritage Centre** (converted mine engine house). At main road, turn **R** through village to return to car park.

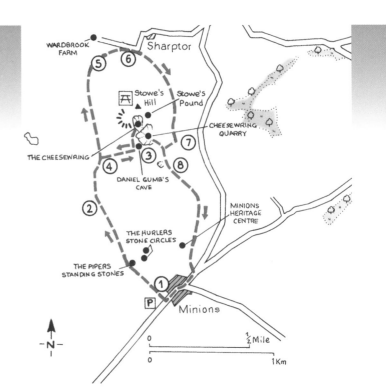

Cardinham Through the Woods

5 miles (8km) 3hrs 30min Ascent: 328ft (100m)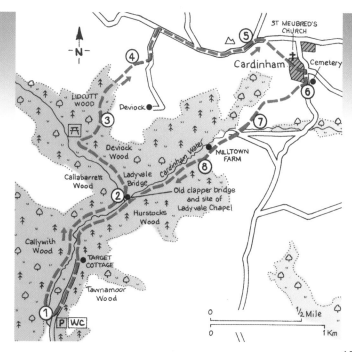

Paths: Generally clear woodland tracks and field sections, 6 stiles

Suggested map: OS Explorer 109 Bodmin Moor

Grid reference: SX 099666

Parking: Cardinham Woods car park

A long woodland walk in quiet countryside between Bodmin town and moor.

① From **Cardinham Woods** car park, head for west side of main bridge over Cardinham Water; bear **R** through wooden barrier to 3-way junction. Keep to **R**; follow track through woods (Cardinham Water on R).

② At junction of tracks, keep **R** and cross hidden tributary stream from L; turn **L** up track. Pass picnic tables by rock face on bend.

③ Turn **R** at junction; pass purple marker post. At next junction, keep ahead along grassy track through **Lidcutt Wood**. Cross stile and on through woods.

④ Enter field; turn sharp **R** and uphill by signpost to gate on to concrete track. Turn **L**; follow track to public road. Turn **R** along road; follow over brow of hill and down into valley.

⑤ Beyond junction, pass public footpath sign, cross river, then go **R** at another public footpath sign. Cross ditch and stile. Head diagonally up field, aiming to **R** of

Cardinham church tower, to stile. Go along grassy ride beside church. Turn **R** at road.

⑥ At public footpath sign opposite **cemetery**, go **R** and through gate into field. Keep parallel to fence; turn **L** in front of house and follow old track, keeping L of tree. Go through wooden gate; keep alongside hedge on R. Where track bends R, turn **L** and downhill between trees; cross meadow to stile. Notices indicate keep to **R-H** edge of field to stile.

⑦ Bear slightly to **L** across next field to wooden gate beside horse jump. Keep ahead through meadow to bridge over stream by water jump; follow path through trees. Go through gate to T-junction with track at **Milltown**. Turn **R**, down surfaced lane; keep **L** at junction. Pass **Milltown Farm**, then junction on L to black-and-white wooden barrier. Go up slope; turn **R** at junction with forestry track.

⑧ Follow track then surfaced lane from **Target Cottage** to car park.

15

Polruan A Glimpse of Old Cornwall

4 miles (6.4km) 3hrs 30min **Ascent:** 754ft (230m)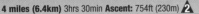

Paths: Good throughout. Can be very muddy in woodland areas during wet weather

Suggested map: OS Explorer 107 St Austell & Liskeard

Grid reference: SX 126511

Parking: Polruan. An alternative start to the walk can be made from the National Trust Pencarrow car park (➤ ❹, SX 149513). You can also park at Fowey's Central car park, then catch the ferry to Polruan

A woodland and coastal walk from Polruan through the ancient parish of Lanteglos.

❶ Walk up from **Quay** at **Polruan**; turn **L** along **East Street**, by telephone box and seat. Go **R**, up steps signposted 'To the Hills' and 'Hall Walk'. Go **L** at next junction, then keep along path ahead. Keep **R** at junction and pass National Trust sign ('North Downs').

❷ Turn **R** at T-junction with track, then shortly bear **L** along path, signposted '**Pont** and **Bodinnick**'. Reach wooden gate on to lane. Don't go through gate but instead bear **L** and go over stile. Follow path, established by National Trust, and eventually descend steep wooden steps.

❸ At T-junction with track, turn **R** and climb uphill. It's worth diverting **L** at T-junction to visit **Pont**. Follow this route to reach lane. Go **L** for short distance then, on bend by Little Churchtown Farm, bear off **R** through gate ('Footpath to Church'). Climb steadily to reach

handsome medieval **Church of St Winwaloe** (or Willow). Novelist Daphne du Maurier was married here in 1932.

❹ Turn **L** outside church and follow narrow lane. At T-junction, just beyond **Pencarrow car park**, cross road and go through gate, then turn **R** along field edge on path established by National Trust, to go through another gate. Turn **L** along field edge.

❺ At field corner, turn **R** on to coast path and descend very steeply. (To continue to Pencarrow Head go **L** over stile here and follow path on to headland. From here coast path can be re-joined and access made to **Great Lantic Beach**.) Follow coast path for about 1¼ miles (2km), keeping to cliff edge and ignoring any junctions.

❻ Where cliff path ends, go through gate to road junction. Cross road then go down School Lane. Turn **R** at 'Speakers Corner', then turn **L** down **Fore Street** to reach **Quay** at **Polruan**.

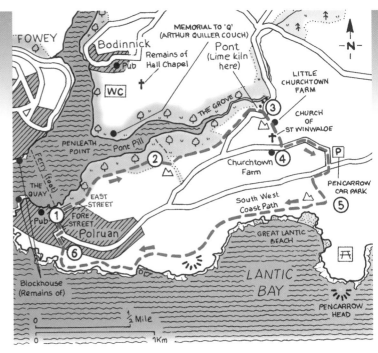

Wadebridge Along the River Camel

6 miles (9.7km) 3hrs 30min **Ascent:** 328ft (100m)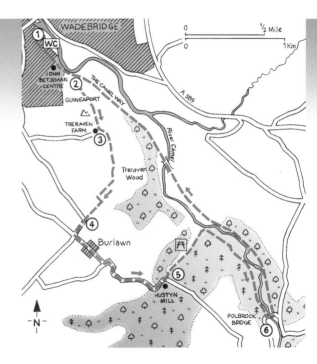

Paths: Farm and forestry tracks and well-surfaced old railway track

Suggested map: OS Explorer 106 Newquay & Padstow

Grid reference: SW 991722

Parking: Wadebridge main car park. Small parking area at end of Guineaport Road at start of the Camel Trail

A gentle woodland walk along the famous old railway trackbed of the Camel Trail and through woodlands.

❶ From car parks in **Wadebridge**, walk along Southern Way Road past **Betjeman Centre**, housed in old railway station, containing memorabilia of famous Poet Laureate, Sir John Betjeman, and continue along Guineaport Road to start of **Camel Way/Trail**. Start from here if adjacent parking is used.

❷ Do not follow the **Camel Way/Trail**. Instead, where road forks just past row of houses, keep **R** and shortly, at junction, where road curves up to **R**, keep ahead along unsurfaced track, signposted 'Public Footpath to Treraven'. Follow track steadily uphill. Go through wooden gate and follow **R-H** field edge to go through another gate. Keep ahead along track to reach junction with wider track. Continue ahead and follow track.

❸ Go **L** in front of **Treraven Farm**, then, in about 15yds (14m), at junction, keep **R** and continue along track to reach bend on minor public road by building.

❹ Keep straight ahead along road, with care, then turn **L** at crossroads, signposted 'Burlawn'. At next junction, go **L** and follow road through little hamlet of Burlawn. Go steeply downhill on narrow lane overshadowed by trees.

❺ At **Hustyn Mill**, beyond little footbridge, turn **L** off road and follow broad woodland track. Stay on main track to where it reaches surfaced road at **Polbrock Bridge**.

❻ Turn **L** over bridge across **River Camel** and, in short distance, go off **L** and down steps to join Camel Trail, which runs through some of Cornwall's most scenic landscape with diversity of animals and bird life. Turn **L** here and follow unwavering line of **Camel Way/Trail** to return to **Wadebridge**.

Fowey Daphne du Maurier's World

7½ miles (12.1km) 4hrs Ascent: 820ft (250m)

Paths: Field paths, rough lanes and coastal footpath, can be very muddy on inland tracks during wet weather, 12 stiles

Suggested map: OS Explorer 107 St Austell & Liskeard

Grid reference: SX 118511

Parking: Readymoney Cove car park, reached by continuing on from entrance to Fowey's main car park

In the footsteps of Daphne du Maurier.

1 From bottom end of car park proceed to walk down St Catherine's Parade; turn **R** towards inlet of **Readymoney Cove**. Continue to end of road, above beach and follow Love Lane uphill (Saints Way). Continue past 1st junction, ignoring options by National Trust sign ('**Covington Woods**').

2 Turn **L** at next junction; climb wooden steps to **Allday's Fields**. Follow **R-H** field edge. At field gap follow track ahead to lane end at **Coombe Farm**. Follow lane ahead.

3 At road, turn **R**; continue to **Lankelly Farm**. Pass junction on R; follow Prickly Post Lane. Shortly turn **L** on to gravel drive; keep **L** and along fenced-in path.

4 Go up rough track by derelict buildings at **Trenant**; cross stile on **L**. Keep ahead alongside field edge; follow path to stile into field below **Tregaminion Farm**. Go up field to gate, continue between buildings;

turn **R**, then **L**, to T-junction with road by entrance gate to **Church of Tregaminion**.

5 Turn **R**; shortly go **L** into field. Reach junction on edge of woods. On main route, keep **L** along field edge and follow coast path to Gribbin Head.

6 Enter wooded National Trust property of Gribbin. Keep **L** at junction. Go through gate and cross to **Gribbin Daymark**. Go **L** and down faint track, then follow coast path to **Polridmouth**.

7 Follow coast path ('**Lankelly Cliff**'). At open ground, follow seaward field edge. Go steeply into, and out of, **Coombe Hawne**. Enter Covington Wood, keep **L** at junction and pass **Rashleigh Mausoleum**.

8 Turn **R** at junction to reach **St Catherine's Castle**. Return along path; go down steps at 1st junction on **R**. Go down wooden steps to **Readymoney Beach**. Return to car park via St Catherine's Parade.

Dodman Point Ancient Walls

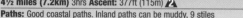

4½ miles (7.2km) 3hrs **Ascent:** 377ft (115m) **②**

Paths: Good coastal paths. Inland paths can be muddy, 9 stiles
Suggested map: OS Explorer 105 Falmouth & Mevagissey
Grid reference: SX 011415
Parking: Gorran Haven car park, pay at kiosk

A circuit of the headland of Dodman Point, with its Iron-Age earthwork.

❶ Turn **L** out of car park and walk down to **Gorran Haven harbour**. Just before access to beach, turn **R** up Fox Hole Lane, then go up steps ('Vault Beach'). Go up more steps, then through gate. Follow coast path ahead, past sign for Lamledra (National Trust).

❷ Keep **L** at junction below rocky outcrop. Alternative path (steep) leads up **R** from here, past memorial plaque, to rejoin main coast path. On main route, go down steps and follow path along slope. At junction, keep **R**. **L-H** track leads down to **Vault Beach**; regain coastal path by another track leading uphill. Keep **L** at next junction.

❸ Go **L** over stile and follow path through scrubland. Keep ahead at junction ('Dodman Point'), then go over stile on to open ground. Continue on footpath to summit of Dodman Point.

❹ On approaching large granite cross on summit of Dodman, reach 1st junction from where path going **R** leads to Watch House. Continue towards cross on summit; just before cross and at next junction and arrow post, go **R** along coast path.

❺ Go over stile beyond gate with access notice pinned to it. Reach junction shortly. Turn **R** and follow path between high banks of **Bulwark**.

❻ Keep ahead where path comes from R. Follow hedged track to kissing gate and lane at Penare. Turn **R** along lane.

❼ At junction leave road and go through field gate ('Treveague'). Keep across 2 fields; at road end by houses, turn **R** ('Gorran Haven'). Go **L** at another signpost then along drive behind house, bearing R. Go **L** through gate and along path above small valley.

❽ Cross muddy area by stepping stones, then go through gate. Follow driveway to T-junction with public road. Turn **R** and walk down (carefully), to Gorran Haven car park.

Nare Head Hidden Cornwall

7 miles (11.3km) 5hrs **Ascent:** 1,312ft (400m) **3**

Paths: Good coastal footpath, field paths and quiet lanes. Field stiles are often overgrown, 30 stiles

Suggested map: OS Explorer 105 Falmouth & Mevagissey

Grid reference: SW 906384

Parking: Carne Beach car park. Large National Trust car park behind beach

A walk through fields and along the coast through remote and endearing landscapes.

❶ Turn **L** out of car park and walk carefully up road. Past steep bend, turn **R**, go up steps and on to coast path. Follow to **Paradoe Cove**; continue past **Nare Head**.

❷ Above **Kiberick Cove**, go through gap in wall. Keep ahead through dip to stile. Follow coast path to **Portloe**. Go **L** up road from cove, past Ship Inn.

❸ Just after sharp L-H bend, where road narrows, cross high step stile to **R**. Cross field to stile; follow next field edge. Pass gate, shortly go **R** and over stile. Cross next field to stile into lane.

❹ Go **R** along road past **Camels Farm** for 200yds (183m), then **L** over stile and follow field edge to another stile. Follow next field edge; just before corner, go **R** over stile. Turn **L** through gap, then diagonally **R** across 2 fields to stile. At road junction, go along road ('Carne and Pendower').

❺ Just past **Tregamenna Manor Farm**, on bend, cross stile by gate. Cut across corner of field, then **R** over stile. Cross next field to stile; continue to T-junction with lane. (Turn **R** to visit **Veryan**.)

❻ Otherwise, turn **L**; just past Churchtown Farm, go **L** over stile. Follow field edge to stile into lane. Go immediately **L** over 2 stiles; follow path, past Carne Beacon, to lane.

❼ At corner junction keep ahead down lane ('Carne Village Only'). Bear **R** down driveway past Beacon Cottage. Go through gate ('Defined Footpaths Nos 44 & 45'). Follow track to **R** between garage and house; follow grassy track, keeping ahead at junction ('**Carne Beach**'). Go through gate (dogs on leads) and follow path alongside bank and fence.

❽ Abreast of gate on R, bear **L** and downhill through scrub (path not evident initially). Soon pick up path leading through gorse to join coast path back to **Carne Beach** and car park.

Bishop's Wood A Forestry Estate

3½ miles (5.7km) 2hrs 30min **Ascent:** 164ft (50m) ⚠

Paths: Forest tracks and paths. Can be very muddy after rain

Suggested map: OS Explorer 105 Falmouth & Mevagissey

Grid reference: SW 820477

Parking: Forestry car park, north of Idless, near Truro. Car park gates are closed at sunset. Working woodland, please take note of notices advising work in progress

Enjoy the local flora and fauna on this gentle stroll through richly diverse woodlands near Truro.

❶ Leave top end of forestry car park at southern end of woods via wooden barrier and go along broad track. In a few paces at fork, keep to **R** fork and follow track above **Woodpark** and along inside edge of Lady's Wood. (Little stream runs below this track which can be very muddy after rain.) Beech trees dominate here and provide good cover. Further into wood you will find that oak, hazel, birch, Japanese larch and holly grow on either side of track that you are walking along.

❷ Keep on main track, parallel to river, ignoring branch tracks leading off to L.

❸ Just before northern end of woodland you reach fork of tracks. Keep on main track as it bends to **L** and uphill. Track levels off and at open area merges with broad forestry ride. Continue walking ahead along this ride.

❹ At forestry notice indicating remains of **Iron-Age encampment**, go **L** along path beneath conifer trees to reach substantial bank and ditch of encampment which is densely covered with coppiced oaks, identified by multiple growths at their base. Mix of broadleaved trees that makes up most of area indicates long-established forestry. Return to main track and turn **L**.

❺ At bend beside wooden bench, where tracks lead off to L and R, go **R** and follow public footpath uphill. At path crossing, turn **L** and follow path through scrubland and young pine trees.

❻ Re-enter mature woodland of **St Clement Wood** and follow track downhill. Keep **R** at junction, then go **L** at next junction. Reach T-junction with broad track. Turn **R** and follow track to car park.

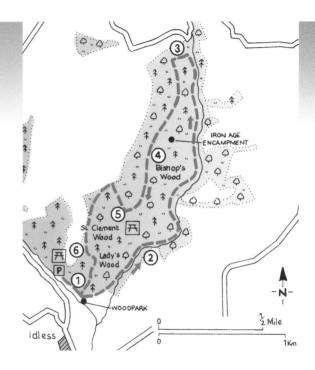

Mylor Churchtown A Waterside Walk

4 miles (6.4km) 3hrs Ascent: 164ft (50m) ⚠️

Paths: Good paths throughout. Wooded section to Trelew Farm is often very wet, 7 stiles

Suggested map: OS Explorer 105 Falmouth & Mevagissey

Grid reference: SW 820352

Parking: Mylor Churchtown car park

To Flushing on a quiet peninsula dominated by ships and sails.

❶ From car park entrance at **Mylor Churchtown**, turn **R** to start of surfaced walkway ('**Flushing**'). Follow walkway; by gateway of house, bear **L** along path ('**Flushing**'). Pass in front of **Restronguet Sailing Club**, go up steps, then **L** along coast path.

❷ Follow path round **Penarrow Point**; continue round Trefusis Point. Reach gate and granite grid stile by wooden shack at **Kilnquay Wood**. Continue to reach lane.

❸ Follow lane **L**; go **R** through gap beside gate and continue along road. Where road drops towards water's edge, bear **R** up slope to '**Bowling Green**'. (Strictly no dog fouling.) Continue past pavilion and toilets and go down walkway; turn **L** by junction and signpost into **Flushing**.

❹ Turn **R** at street junction; go along Trefusis Road past Seven Stars Inn. At junction by Royal Standard Inn, keep **R** past Post Office; go up Kersey Road. At top, by **Orchard Vale**, go **L** up steps ('**Mylor Church**'). Cross stile; keep to field edge to house and stile.

❺ Go **R** through gate, then turn **L** over cattle grid and follow drive to **Penarrow Road**. Cross carefully, go down road opposite, then **R** down steps and on down field edge. Keep ahead where field edge bends **L** to reach woods.

❻ Enter woodland; keep **R** at junction to follow rocky path (often mini stream after heavy rainfall). Go through gate, keep **L** at junction, then cross proper stream. Go through tiny gate; turn **R** down farm track to surfaced lane at **Trelew**.

❼ Turn **R** along lane, passing old water pump. At slipway, keep ahead along Wayfield Road. Continue between granite posts and on to public road into Mylor Churchtown. Cross road with care (blind corner); go through churchyard of St Mylor Church (not public right of way). Turn **R** at waterfront to find car park.

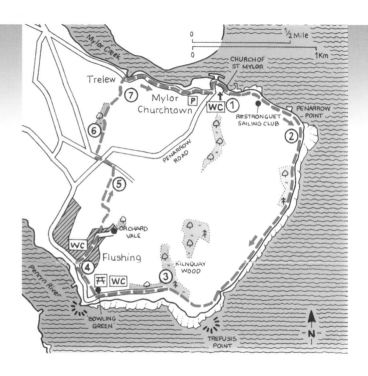

St Agnes High Cliffs and a High Hill

5 miles (8km) 3hrs **Ascent:** 623ft (190m)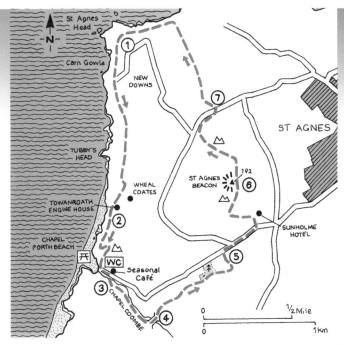

Paths: Good coastal footpaths and inland tracks

Suggested map: OS Explorer 104 Redruth & St Agnes

Grid reference: SW 699512

Parking: St Agnes Head. Number of parking spaces along the clifftop track. Start the walk from any of these

A bracing walk along the cliffs at St Agnes, then inland to the top of St Agnes Beacon.

1 Join coastal footpath from wherever you park along cliff top. Follow stony track across little promontory of **Tubby's Head**, former Iron-Age settlement. Branch off **R** on to narrower path about 100yds (90m) before old mine buildings (these are remains of **Wheal Coates** mine). Cross stone stile and continue to **Towanroath mine engine house**.

2 About 50yds (46m) beyond **Towanroath** branch off **R** at signpost and descend to **Chapel Porth Beach**.

3 Cross stream at back corner of car park and follow path up **Chapel Combe** next to stream. Pass below mine building and where path forks among trees, go **L** through wooden kissing gate.

4 Cross bridge then turn **R** onto track. Continue along grassy track and where track narrows, keep ahead at fork. Keep alongside field and on to track; turn **L** over wooden stile by gate onto track. After around 50yds (46m), reach junction with wide track. Turn **L** and continue to public road.

5 Turn **R** along public road, and keep ahead at junction. In 200yds (183m), next to entrance to **Sunholme Hotel**, continue up stony track on **L**. After 50yds (46m), at junction, go **L** and follow path rising to obvious summit of 629ft (192m) **St Agnes Beacon**, used traditionally for lighting of signal fires and for celebratory bonfires. Views from top of **Beacon** reach as far as tors of Bodmin Moor.

6 From summit of **Beacon** follow lower of 2 tracks, heading northwest, down towards road. Just before you reach road turn **R** along narrow path, skirting base of hill, eventually emerging at road by seat.

7 Cross over and follow track opposite, across New Downs, directly to edge of cliffs, then turn **L** at junction with coast path and return to car park.

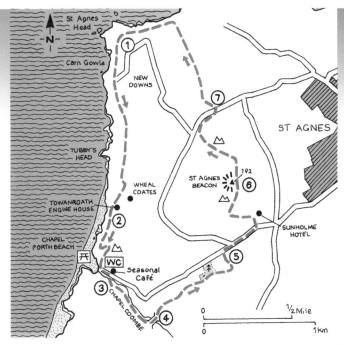

13 Redruth Mines and Methodism

4 miles (6.4km) 2hrs 30min Ascent: 442ft (135m)

Paths: Field paths, rough tracks and surfaced lanes. Can be muddy after rain, 6 stiles

Suggested map: OS Explorer 104 Redruth & St Agnes

Grid reference: SW 699421

Parking: Several car parks in Redruth

A walk through Cornwall's mining heartland, visiting Gwennap Pit.

❶ From any of car parks, go to **Fore Street**. Walk up to 3-way junction (railway station to R) and take Wesley Street (middle branch) to **L** of Redruth Methodist Church ('To Victoria Park'). Shortly turn **R** (**Sea View Terrace**); **Pednandrea Mine** chimney stack is up to L along road. Pass Basset Street (R); where streets cross, go **L** up **Raymond Road** to T-junction with **Sandy Lane**.

❷ Cross road carefully; follow track opposite, ('Public Bridleway' and '**Grambler Farm**'). Go through gate by farm; continue to open area. Bear **L** following much narrower track between hedges. At junction with another track turn **L** ('Gwennap Pit').

❸ Go **R**, following **Gwennap Pit** signposts; cross stile by gate, then go through small wooden gate. Keep ahead (free-ranging pigs may be in area; dogs under strict control). Cross stile at next gate; follow

field edge ahead. Cross final field towards house, then walk down lane past house to junction of surfaced roads at **Busveal**. Cross and follow road opposite to **Gwennap Pit**.

❹ Follow road away from **Gwennap Pit**. Turn off to **R** along broad track ('Public Bridleway'). Keep ahead at 2 crossings; at final crossing beside ruined building, turn **R** and follow stony track up hill to **Carn Marth**.

❺ Pass flooded quarry (viewpoint far side); just beyond trig point, bear **R** on path alongside fenced-in rim of deep quarry. At surfaced lane, turn **L**, **L** again at next junction, then follow lane to T-junction with road at **Calhill Farm**. Turn **R**; walk along **Sandy Road** (watch for traffic) for 275yds (251m).

❻ Go **L** at junction ('cycle route'); follow lane **R**, then **L** into avenue of houses. At crossroads turn **R** (Trefusis Road). At next junction turn **L** (**Raymond Road**), then **R** (**Sea View Terrace**). Turn **L** down Wesley Street and on into **Fore Street**.

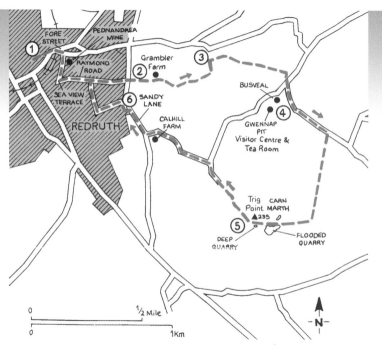

Helford Hidden Creeks

5 miles (8km) 3hrs **Ascent:** 328ft (100m) ▲

Paths: Good woodland paths and tracks and field paths. Short section of quiet lane, 10 stiles

Suggested map: OS Explorer 103 The Lizard

Grid reference: SW 759261

Parking: Helford car park. Large car park overlooking creek. Can become busy in summer. Only authorised cars are allowed beyond the car park into the village of Helford

A circuit of peaceful tidal creeks.

1 On leaving car park, turn **L** along path ('Coast Path'). Go through metal gate; follow sunken track. Descend steps, then turn **R** along lane. At steep R-H bend, bear ahead along track. Follow path through trees, keeping **L** at any junctions.

2 Leave wooded area via metal gate, then turn **L** along field edge to stile. Follow bottom edge of next 2 fields. Cross fence at field gap beside white pole and red post and triangle (navigation marks). Follow field edge. Go through kissing gate, then follow field edge (seat and viewpoint on L), to where it ends at beginning of wide track (to make short circuit of **Dennis Head**, follow track ahead to stile on L).

3 To continue on main route, turn **R** at start of wide track; follow L-H field edge and then path across open field. Join track behind house, then go through kissing gate and descend to **St Anthony's Church**. Follow

road alongside **Gillan Creek**.

4 Just beyond where road curves round bay, go up **R** between granite gate posts by public footpath sign. Follow broad track through trees to houses at **Roscaddon**. Keep ahead along track leading to Manaccan at T-junction opposite Manaccan church.

5 Go through churchyard and on through gate opposite to road (village shop L). Keep ahead to junction (**New Inn** L), then go up **R**, past school. Keep uphill, then turn **L** along Minster Meadow, cross stile, and through 2 fields to reach road.

6 Go diagonally **L** to stile opposite, cross field, then go **L** following signposts to woods. Follow path ahead. At junction keep ahead, cross stile and reach 2nd junction.

7 Bear down **R** following broad track through trees to buildings at Helford. Keep ahead at surfaced road and follow road uphill to car park.

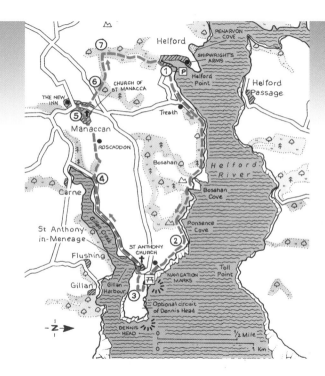

Cadgwith The Serpentine Route

4½ miles (7.2km) 3hrs Ascent: 230ft (70m)

Paths: Very good. Occasionally rocky in places. Rock can be slippery when wet
Suggested map: OS Explorer 103 The Lizard
Grid reference: SW 720146
Parking: Cadgwith car park. About 350yds (320m) from Cadgwith. Busy in summer

A wandering route between coast and countryside through the serpentine landscape of the Lizard Peninsula.

1 Go **L** along grassy ride below car park, to stile. Continue over another stile, then branch **R**. Turn **R** at lane, then on corner, go up track and continue to main road at little village of **Ruan Minor**.

2 Go **L** and, just beyond shop, turn **L** down surfaced path. Rejoin main road by thatched cottage (there are toilets just before road). Cross diagonally **R**, then go down lane past **Church of St Ruan** (small building of mainly local serpentine stone).

3 Just past old mill and bridge, go **R** at T-junction to reach car park at Poltesco. From far end of car park follow track, signposted '**Carleon Cove**'. Go **R** at junction.

4 Turn **L** at T-junction just above cove (once site of water wheels, steam engines, machine shops and factory where serpentine was processed), and again

turn **L** where path branches in about ¼ mile (400m). Continue along cliff-edge path to archetypal Cornish village of **Cadgwith**.

5 Follow narrow path, signposted 'Coast Path'. By house gateway, go **L** up surfaced path ('**Devil's Frying Pan**'). At an open area turn **L**, pass Townplace Cottage, cross meadow and reach **Devil's Frying Pan** itself, vast gulf in cliffs caused by collapse of section of coast undermined by sea.

6 At junction, just past chalet studio, follow path inland to T-junction with rough track. Turn **L** and, at public lane, go **L** again to reach entrance to **Church of Holy Cross** standing on raised ground at **Grade**, after 1 mile (1.6km).

7 Follow edge of field behind church, then cross next field to reach lane. Ancient **St Ruan's Well** is opposite diagonally L. Turn **R** for 200yds (183m), then branch off **R** between stone pillars to return to car park.

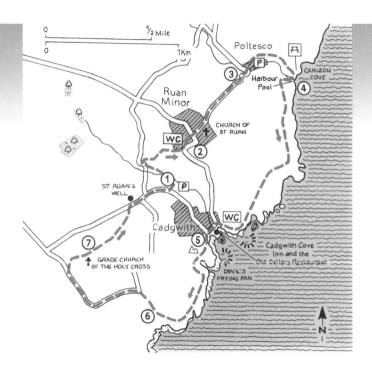

Portreath Cliffs and Deep Woods

4 miles (6.4km) 3hrs **Ascent:** 459ft (140m)

Paths: Good coastal path, woodland path, farm tracks
Suggested map: OS Explorer 104 Redruth & St Agnes
Grid reference: SW 656453
Parking: Portreath Beach

Along spectacular cliffs and through woods.

❶ Turn **R** outside **Portreath Beach** car park, cross bridge and turn **R** up **Battery Hill** ('Coast Path'). Follow lane uphill to houses above beach. Go **L** in front of garage ('North Coast Foot Path').

❷ Follow path through gate; keep straight uphill to cliff top (take care). Turn **L** to wooden gate; follow path round cliff edge above **Ralph's Cupboard**. Continue by steep paths into and out of **Porth-cadjack Cove**.

❸ At car parking area above **Basset's Cove** follow broad track inland. At road, cross and turn **L** for 40yds (37m); watch for fast-moving traffic. Reach granite grid stile on **R**, cross stile. Follow narrow path into **Tehidy Woods**.

❹ Keep ahead at crossing. Soon pass R-H junction, then L-H junction ('Pedestrians Only'). Keep straight ahead to reach T-junction with broad track. Turn **L**.

❺ Reach junction and 4-way signpost beside 2 seats (café ¼ mile/400m down R-H signposted track). On main route, keep ahead ('East Lodge'). Reach junction by seat. Go **R** and through wooden kissing gate. Cross golf course (watch for golf balls). Go through metal kissing gate; follow track by **golf course**.

❻ Shortly beyond end of **golf course** section, bear **L** into woods by staggered wooden barrier, ('Pedestrians Only'). Stay on main path, ignoring side paths, then bear **R** to car park and public road. Cross diagonally **R**, then go **L** between wooden posts (red marks). Follow track ahead (often muddy).

❼ Go **R** on to wider track by field gate. Next section can be muddy in rain. Pass holiday chalets and reach T-junction above farm buildings (**Feadon Farm**).

❽ Turn **L**, then shortly **R** down track. At farmyard go sharp **L** by public footpath sign; follow path through woods to surfaced road. Past 'Glenfeadon Castle' turn **L** (**Glenfeadon Terrace**), pass beneath bridge, then at junction keep ahead (Tregea Terrace) and return to **Portreath Beach** car park.

Mullion Cove Wildflower Haven

7 miles (11.3km) 4hrs **Ascent:** 164ft (50m)

Paths: Good inland tracks and paths, can be muddy during wet weather. Coastal footpath, 21 stiles

Suggested map: OS Explorer 103 The Lizard

Grid reference: SW 669162

Parking: Predannack Wollas Farm car park (National Trust)

The Lizard Peninsula heathland supports some of Britain's most remarkable wild flowers.

1 Leave **Predannack Wollas Farm** car park by bottom end. Follow winding track ahead for just under ½ mile (800m) to gate. (Ignore signposted track L just before gate.) Beyond gate, bear **L** to stile. Follow edge of next field to stile; continue to open ground by gate in fence on **R**.

2 Cross stile next to gate; bear away from fence along path to English Nature's Kynance Farm Nature Reserve. Keep ahead towards distant buildings.

3 Watch for gap in hedge on **L**, go through, then cross field to rough track. Turn **R** along track then bear **L** and follow edge of scrub.

4 Go through gate; follow track **R**. Merge with another track; just before ford, bear **R** along track towards coast (**Kynance Farm** R).

5 At crossing with coast path, go **R** and uphill; cross stile on to cliff top. Follow coast path round edge of cliffs at **Pengersick** and **Vellan Head**.

6 Go **L** at junction, just past National Trust sign ('**Predannack**'). (You can return to car park by following inland path from here.) Cross stream in dip; climb up **L**, then continue along coast path to **Mullion Cove** and **Harbour**.

7 Go up road from **Mullion Harbour**; beyond public toilets and shop, turn **R** at coast path sign. Keep to **R** of entrance to holiday residential site; follow track uphill. On bend and just before granite pillar, go **R** and over stone stile. Follow path ahead through thorn tree grove, then through fields.

8 Pass tall granite cross, then reach lane. Turn **R** along lane towards farm. Before **Predannack Manor Farm** entrance, go **L** over stile by field gate, then **R** along field edge. Cross stile, then **L** along hedged-in path; cross stile and 2 fields to lane (watch for traffic). Turn **R** to **Lower Predannack Wollas Farm** car park.

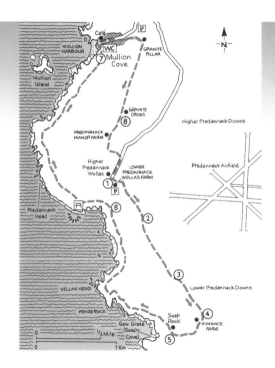

Prussia Cove The Smuggler King

4 miles (6.4km) 3hrs Ascent: 394ft (120m)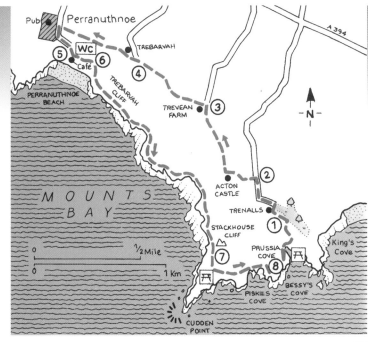

Paths: Good field paths and coastal paths, 18 stiles

Suggested map: OS Explorer 102 Land's End

Grid reference: SW 554282

Parking: Trenalls, Prussia Cove. Small privately owned car park. Or car park at Perranuthnoe, from where the walk can be started at Point ⑤

Through the coastal domain of John Carter, the famous Cornish smuggler.

① From car park entrance walk back along approach road, past large house (watch for traffic). After 2nd bend, by camp site entrance, look for stile on **L**, past field gate.

② Cross stile; follow field edge, bearing **R**, where it bends **L**, to stile in hedge opposite. Walk down edge of next field, behind **Acton Castle** (private dwellings); turn **R** along field edges to stile into adjacent lane. Turn **R**.

③ Turn **L** along track at junction in front of bungalow entrance at **Trevean Farm**. At L-H bend go on to stony track for short distance; at public footpath sign, ascend to **R**, up narrow steps, then **L** along field edge.

④ At **Trebarvah**, cross farm lane, pass in front of barns (view of St Michael's Mount ahead), then follow field edge to hedged-in path. Follow path ahead through fields, then pass houses to reach main road

opposite **Victoria Inn**. Go **L** and follow road to car park above **Perranuthnoe Beach**.

⑤ For beach and **Cabin Café**, keep ahead. On main route, go **L**, just beyond car park, and along lane. Bear **R** at fork, then **R** again just past house at junction.

⑥ Go down track towards sea and follow it **L**. At field entrance, go down **R** (signposted), turn sharp **L** through gap and follow coast path along edge of **Trebarvah** and **Stackhouse Cliffs**.

⑦ At National Trust property of Cudden Point, follow path uphill, then across inner slope of headland above **Piskies Cove**.

⑧ Go through gate and pass ancient fishing huts. Follow path round edge of **Bessy's Cove** inlet of **Prussia Cove**, to track by thatched cottage. Cove can be reached down path on **R** just before this junction. Turn **R** and follow track, keeping **L** at junctions, to return to car park.

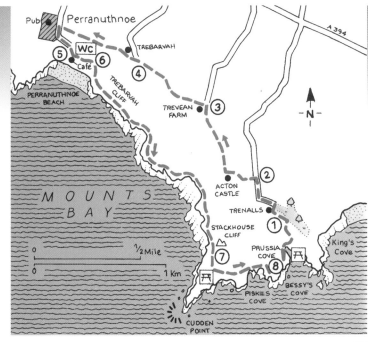

Lamorna Cove Merry Maidens

6 miles (9.7km) 3hrs 30min **Ascent:** 558ft (170m) ⚠

Paths: Good coastal footpaths, field paths and rocky tracks

Suggested map: OS Explorer 102 Land's End

Grid reference: SW 450241

Parking: Lamorna Cove

A coastal and inland walk passing an ancient stone circle along the way.

❶ From far end of seaward car park, at end of terrace above **Lamorna Cove**, follow coast path through short rocky sections. Continue along path past tops of **Tregurnow Cliff** and **Rosemodress Cliff**.

❷ Pass above entrance ramp and steps to **Tater-du Lighthouse**. Pass large residence (R); where track bends R, keep **L** along coast path, at signpost.

❸ Descend steeply (care when muddy) from **Boscawen Point** to **St Loy's Cove**. Cross section of boulders (may be slippery when wet). Follow path inland through dense vegetation and by stream. Cross private drive then climb steeply uphill. Cross stile on to track, turn **R** over stile and follow path through trees.

❹ By wooden signpost and old tree, go **R** and cross stream on large boulders; follow hedged-in path **L**. Shortly, by wooden signpost, go **R** and up to surfaced lane. Turn **L**; follow lane uphill. At junction with bend on another track, keep ahead and uphill. At **Boskenna Farm** buildings follow lane **L**; keep ahead.

❺ From lane, at entrance drive to bungalow on R, right of way goes through field gate, then cuts across field corner to stile in wire fence. Beyond, right of way (no path) leads diagonally across field to top **R-H** corner, where stile leads into lay-by with granite **cross** at edge. An alternative route is to continue along farm lane; turn **R** along public road, taking care, to lay-by.

❻ Follow road to **Tregiffian burial chamber** on R, then **Merry Maidens** stone circle. From circle continue to field corner, cross stile and follow path diagonally **R** across next field towards buildings. Cross stile on to road, then down **R-H** of 2 lanes (surfaced, 'No Through Road' sign).

❼ Where lane ends, keep ahead on to public bridleway. Follow track downhill to public road. Turn **R** and walk down road, with care, passing Lamorna Wink Inn, to car park.

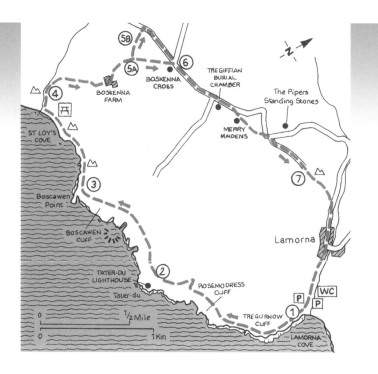

Porthcurno Golden Beaches and Cliffs

3½ miles (5.7km) 2hrs 30min **Ascent:** 164ft (50m)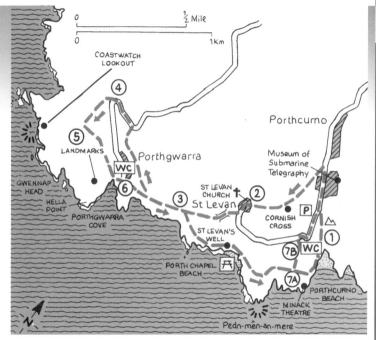

Paths: Coastal footpath

Suggested map: OS Explorer 107 St Austell & Liskeard

Grid reference: SW 384224

Parking: Porthcurno, St Levan and Porthgwarra

Between sandy coves and granite cliffs on the Land's End Peninsula.

❶ From car park, walk back up approach road; just beyond Porthcurno Hotel, turn **L** along track and follow to cottages. Pass to their **R** and go through kissing gate. Follow field path past granite cross.

❷ Enter **St Levan churchyard** by granite stile. Go round far side of church to entrance gate and on to surfaced lane; cross and follow path opposite ('**Porthgwarra Cove**'). Cross footbridge over stream; shortly, at junction, take **R** fork and follow path to merge with main coast path and keep ahead.

❸ After path begins to descend towards **Porthgwarra Cove**, branch **R** up wooden steps. Reach track and turn up **R**, then at road, **L**.

❹ Go round sharp L–H bend; at footpath signpost, go **R** down path and cross stone footbridge. Continue uphill to reach bend on track, just up from granite houses.

❺ Turn **L**, cross stile beside gate, then down surfaced lane to **Porthgwarra Cove**. Opposite shop and café, go **R** down track ('Coast Path'); follow path **L** in front of house. Go **R** at junction and climb steps.

❻ Continue along coast path, partly reversing previous route past Point ❸. Keep **R** at junctions; eventually descend past **St Levan's Well** to just above **Porth Chapel Beach**. (Control dogs on beach.) Follow coast path steeply over **Pedn-mên-an-mere**; continue to **Minack Theatre** car park.

❼ For surefooted walkers, cross car park and go down track to **L** of Minack compound; descend steep cliff steps (take care). When path levels off, continue to junction. **R** fork leads to Porthcurno Beach and back to car park. Continuation leads to road opposite Beach Café, where **R** turn leads to car park. For less challenging alternative, turn **L** out of Minack car park. Follow approach road to T-junction with public road. Turn **R** and walk down road, watching out for traffic.

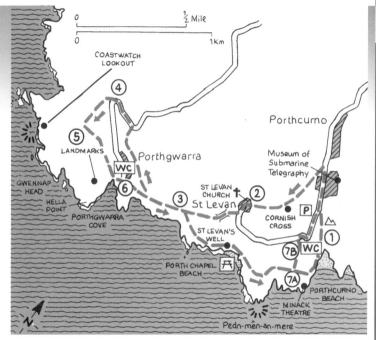

Colyton A Chequered History

4¼ miles (6.8km) 2hrs 30min **Ascent:** 197ft (60m)

Paths: Fields and country lanes, one narrow boggy track, 9 stiles

Suggested map: OS Explorer 116 Lyme Regis & Bridport

Grid reference: SY 245940

Parking: Paying car park in centre of Colyton (Dolphin Street)

Along the River Coly and Umborne Brook.

❶ From car park turn **R**, then 1st **L** (Lower Church Street). Turn **L** at Gerrard Arms (Rosemary Lane), **R** (Vicarage Street), then **R** towards river; cross bridge.

❷ Turn **L** through kissing gate and along river bank on **East Devon Way** (EDW). Follow path through 2 kissing gates. Ignore next footpath sign R; go ahead through 2 gates, following river.

❸ At junction of footpaths at end of field keep river **L**; take kissing gate in corner on to concrete walkway. Go through kissing gate and across field to 2 gates and footbridge below 3 oaks. Cross another footbridge/gate to bridge over river on **L**.

❹ Turn **R**, through gate to lane; turn **R**. At **Cadhayne Farm** (R) turn **L** through gate opposite farmyard. Walk uphill, through gate at top and straight on. Lane veers L; turn **R** along muddy path, to road ('Tritchayne').

❺ Cross; walk downhill along **Watery Lane**. At **Tritchmarsh**, lane becomes grassy track; follow

footpath sign **R** on wooden walkway. Go **L** to gate and **L** round field. Ignore next stile L; take small gate/bridge/gate to **R**; cross paddock and **Umborne Brook** via gate and walkway to **Lexhayne Mill**. Path runs to kissing gate and over stile in wire fence. Cross next stile; head diagonally **R** for drive to **Lexhayne Farm**. Go **L**, then **R** (signed) through hedge gap.

❻ Cross diagonally down field towards bottom corner, over double gate/bridge and footbridge over brook. Walk **L**; cross stile; cross brook via double gate/footbridge with **Colyton church** ahead.

❼ Aim for stile in fence ahead **R**. Keep ahead; cross brook via double gate/bridge, then **L**. Cross stile and 2 stiles/footbridges, then diagonally across upper part of next field. Cross stile, go downhill; over stile to road.

❽ Turn **L**; pass picnic area at **Road Green**, then over bridge. Take 1st **L** (Vicarage Street); go straight on, past church (L), through town centre and down Silver Street to car park.

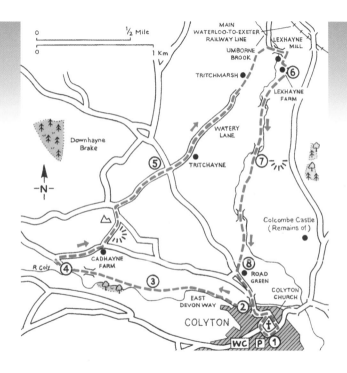

Broadhembury An Unspoilt Village

5½ miles (8.8km) 2hrs 30min **Ascent:** 360ft (110m)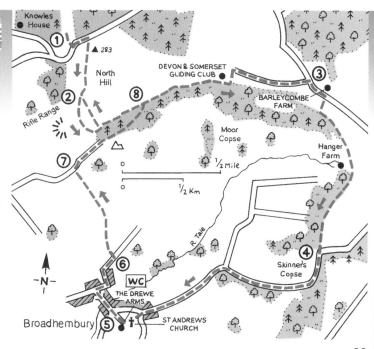

Paths: Country lanes, pastures and woodland paths, 7 stiles
Suggested map: OS Explorer 115 Exeter & Sidmouth
Grid reference: SY 095068
Parking: Unsurfaced car park at Knowles Wood

Beech woods and rolling farmland around an unspoilt thatched village.

❶ Return to road; turn **L** uphill. Shortly bridleway sign points **R** through another parking area, then path reaches signpost and metal gate (L), indicating you have reached **Devon & Somerset Gliding Club**. Ignore gate; continue on bridleway.

❷ Pass through next metal gate on to airfield. Turn **R** along edge, keeping to R of clubhouse. Follow tarmac drive **L** over cattle grid and down lane to road.

❸ Turn **R**; pass **Barleycombe Farm** (L), then follow bridleway signs **R** through gate, **L** through another and into field. Follow track along bottom of field. Path curves **R** through beech trees and metal gate, then runs straight across next field towards beech tree and gate. Take track through gate. Shortly bear **R** along grassy path (ignore gate ahead) and through 2 metal gates (coniferous plantation to R).

❹ Path ends at lane; turn **R** downhill into **Broadhembury**. At **St Andrew's Church** cross road and go through churchyard, then under lychgate and downhill to **Drewe Arms** on your L.

❺ From pub, turn **L** down main street to bridge and ford. Turn **R** up lane, past playground and up hill.

❻ Past 2 thatched cottages go **L** over stile in hedge and up field, aiming for stile in top **L** corner. Go over and ahead, keeping old farmhouse and barn to R. Cross next stile, then another. Turn **R**, round edge of field, and over small stile into small copse. Another stile leads into next field; look across to locate next stile in beech hedge opposite, which leads to green lane.

❼ Turn **R**; walk uphill between conifers (**L**), and fields until metal gate leads on to open gateway and back on to airfield.

❽ Turn **L** along edge of field. Go **R** over 2nd iron gate to rejoin bridleway which leads back to road. Turn **L** downhill to your car.

Bickleigh The Exe Valley Way

4¼ miles (6.8km) 2hrs **Ascent:** 509ft (155m) **2**

Paths: Country lanes, one long, steep, muddy track

Suggested map: OS Explorer 114 Exeter & the Exe Valley

Grid reference: SX 939075

Parking: Bickleigh Mill just off A396 at Bickleigh Bridge

Leave the crowds behind at Bickleigh Bridge and explore the lovely Exe Valley.

❶ From public parking area at edge of **Bickleigh Mill** go back, with care, to A396 and cross bridge. Turn **L** down A3072, following brown tourist sign (**Bickleigh Castle**). Take 1st lane **L**, running along edge of flood plain on **Exe Valley Way** (EVW). **Bickleigh Castle** is R. Go straight on past **Way Farm**.

❷ Just after **Way Farm** buildings turn **R** to leave **Exe Valley Way** ('Lee Cross & Perry Farm'). Take care here as this is a very narrow lane, carrying busy traffic, especially from local working farms. This ancient lane climbs steeply uphill and after 700yds (640m) comes to farm at **Lee Cross**.

❸ Immediately after house keep straight ahead along road. Pass **Perry Farm** and continue until you reach T-junction; turn **L** on to green lane. Continue down this lane until you reach another T-junction. Turn **R**; lane levels off and becomes easier.

❹ Where green lane meets tarmac lane turn **L** and proceed steeply downhill (EVW). Views over River Exe and Silverton church beyond are glorious. Follow lane down until you see **Tray Mill Farm** on L.

❺ Way home is straight on along lane, but it's worth doing small detour to river. Turn **R** through farmyard (no sign) and pass through metal gate on to concrete standing. Ahead is suspension bridge over river; cross it and go straight on to reach dismantled railway track. Do not turn **L** along track – which would take you straight back to your car – it's privately owned and has no public right of way.

❻ Path goes straight on here to meet A369. Turn **L**, then **R** to walk through **Bickleigh** village back to mill (road is busy; it's better to retrace steps to **Tray Mill Farm** and take quieter route back to **Bickleigh Mill**).

❼ Back on lane by **Tray Mill Farm**, turn **R** and walk along lane, past **Bickleigh Castle**, turning **R** at A3072, and **R** again over bridge to return to your car.

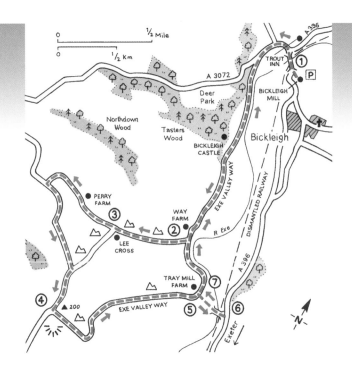

Otterton Bird Life at the Reserve

4¼ miles (6.8km) 2hrs **Ascent:** 164ft (50m)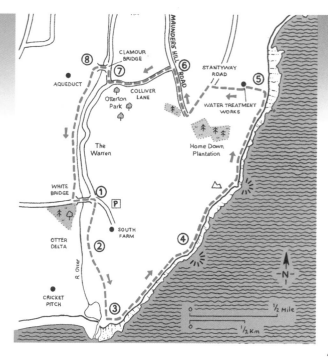

Paths: Good level paths, coastal section and lanes, 2 stiles
Suggested map: OS Explorer 115 Exeter & Sidmouth
Grid reference: SX 077830
Parking: By side of broad, quiet lane near entrance to South Farm

Along the River Otter towards High Peak.

❶ Walk through kissing gate to **R** of gate to **South Farm**. Turn **R** following signs ('Coast Path Ladram Bay'). Sandy path runs along field edge (views R over saltmarshes of Otter Estuary Nature Reserve and River Otter).

❷ At end of field shallow flight of wooden steps leads to walkway and footbridge, and up into next field (good views downriver to shingle bank at Budleigh Salterton).

❸ Path continues gently downhill until it turns sharply **L** following line of coast.

❹ After 1 mile (1.6km) path rises; ahead is Lyme Bay, including High Peak (564ft/157m – one of highest points on South Devon coast). Follow coast path: red sandstone cliffs extremely friable and 'chunks' continually tumble seawards, but path is safe. Pass through small gate by ruined lookout building, and downhill.

❺ Turn **L** to leave coast path on 'Permissive path to Otterton'; this leads over stile; turn immediately **L** and follow path **R** around **water treatment works**, and up gravelly lane to **Stantyway Road**. Lane veers R, but turn **L** up grassy track, following signs to Otterton and **River Otter**. Track soon veers R and gives way to tarmac lane.

❻ After 400yds (366m) **Colliver Lane** and **River Otter** signed to L. Turn **L** here; follow narrow, wooded green lane, which ends at gate. Go through, then almost immediately another; follow signs along edge of next field, which you leave over stile on to track.

❼ Turn immediately **L** between 2 brick pillars, then **R** under large oak tree. Descend steps and cross **River Otter** on Clamour Bridge (wooden footbridge).

❽ Turn **L** and follow river south; over small leat (look out for aqueduct coming across meadows on R), through gate and continue to White Bridge; go through kissing gate, turn **L** and find your car.

Killerton The National Trust

4¼ miles (6.8km) 2hrs 15min **Ascent:** 131ft (40m)

Paths: Good footpaths, bridleways and farm tracks, 3 stiles

Suggested map: OS Explorer 114 Exeter & the Exe Valley

Grid reference: SX 977001

Parking: National Trust car park plus overflow car park

Around the Killerton Estate.

1 From car park return to road and turn **R** to gate and cattle grid at entrance drive to **Killerton House**. Follow public footpath sign towards house, passing stables and courtyard on R.

2 Leave main approach drive as it gets closer to **Killerton House**. Pass house on **R-H** side. Continue straight on, past walled gardens and ornamental lawns. Shortly after, cross stile on **R**; continue through small gate in hedge ahead to large sloping field.

3 Turn **R** uphill, keeping by hedge, then metal fence on R. At top of field ignore public footpath sign ('Bluebell Gate'); turn **L** down across field to enter **Columbjohn Wood** through gate ('Beware of walkers').

4 Take bridlepath **L**, and immediately branch **L** on higher path, leading gradually downhill. Leave wood by another gate; keep straight on to meet and follow farm track. After 250yds (229m) cross stile on **R** to enter field. Keeping wood on R, pass cottage to 16th-century **Columbjohn Chapel**.

5 Cross another stile to grassy drive opposite chapel; look at old gatehouse archway. Retrace steps through field back to farm track.

6 Turn **L** and follow track through woods and fields around edge of estate. **River Culm** is on L, but you will be more aware of main **Penzance-to-Paddington railway**. Track reaches road by **Ellerhayes Bridge**.

7 Do not go on to road; turn **R** to follow edge of parkland and woods, keeping road on L. Pass through several gates ('National Trust bridlepath') to join gravel track which passes entrance to **Chapel of Holy Evangelists**, built in Norman style in 1842 for Acland family, their tenants and employees, and to replace one at Columbjohn.

8 Continue on to road. Turn **R** through cutting, and again branch **R**, following signs to Killerton House, to reach car park.

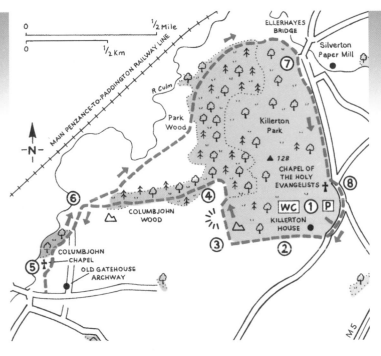

Withleigh Watching for Buzzards

3¾ miles (6km) 2hrs Ascent: 150ft (45m)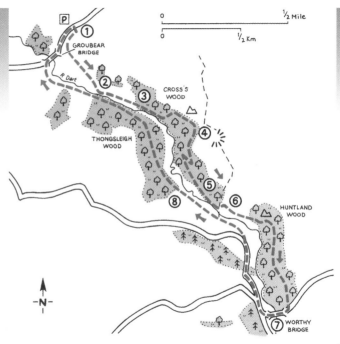

Paths: Waymarked paths, tracks and quiet lanes, 3 stiles

Suggested map: OS Explorer 114 Exeter & the Exe Valley

Grid reference: SX 905121

Parking: A narrow lane (No Through Road) leads to car park from B3137 near sign to Withleigh church

A walk through peaceful hillside woods and along river banks.

❶ From car park cross stile into field, and turn **R**. At hedge ahead turn **L** and walk towards wood. Drop down steeply **R**, heading for gate and stone water trough near by.

❷ Once through gate go ahead, keeping hedge **L**. Cross next stile and continue with tiny River Dart on **R**. Before bridge turn **L** at waymarker, through small gate into another field. Turn **R**, keeping high hedge **R**.

❸ Leave field through next gate on to broad track which rises through **Cross's Wood**. Soon after passing bench, waymarker directs you **L**, off track and back into woods up steep path (overgrown and muddy in places). Continue to climb to wide track at top of woods.

❹ Turn **R** to follow track gently downhill, through gate into open area where it zig-zags more steeply downhill between gorse, broom and bracken.

❺ Continue on to valley bottom and join riverside track, passing through gate with sign asking horse-riders to dismount. Before bridge ahead turn **L** on broad track. Shortly turn **R** over stile and double-plank bridge to enter field.

❻ Keep high hedge to **L** and walk through field to reach small gate into Huntland Wood. Follow path steeply uphill. Path levels off and leads through beautiful upper part of wood before descending gradually to leave at lane.

❼ Turn **R** and go downhill, cross River Dart at **Worthy Bridge**, turn **R** at next junction and past some houses. Where lane bends **L**, go ahead through gate on to track; follow track (river to **R**) through gate and into **Thongsleigh Wood**.

❽ Continue along track, with river **R**. At gate leave wood and enter meadows; path is faint here but continues ahead. Next gate (rather decrepit) leads on to lane. Turn **R** over **Groubear Bridge** and climb back up ancient rocky lane to car park.

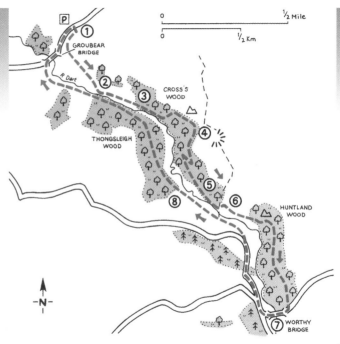

Brampford Speke The Meandering Exe

3½ miles (5.7km) 1hr 30min **Ascent:** Negligible

Paths: Grassy field paths, tracks and country lanes, 5 stiles

Suggested map: OS Explorer 114 Exeter & the Exe Valley

Grid reference: SX 927986

Parking: On laneside near St Peter's Church, Brampford Speke

Water-meadows, ox-bow lakes and herons.

❶ Follow **Exe Valley Way** (EVW) footpath signs through churchyard to **L** of church. Leave via metal gate; follow path through kissing gate and on to lane at kissing gate under lychgate.

❷ Turn **R** and follow footpath signs downhill; cross River Exe over wooden bridge. Turn **L** across meadow, following footpath signs. Ignore footpath signpost pointing R; go through gateway in hedge, keeping close to river (on L).

❸ Follow river as it loops around flood plain. Cross old railway line via 2 kissing gates (old railway bridge piers in river on L).

❹ Immediately through 2nd gate drop down **L** to river; continue straight on. Cross stile, then double stile, then 2nd double stile with plank bridge.

❺ After 1 mile (1.6km) path veers R away from river and down green lane to kissing gate. Turn immediately **L** along another green lane. At next footpath post go

R, then straight on (ignoring EVW signs L) along green lane, which crosses arable farmland, ending at road on edge of Rewe.

❻ Turn **R** along lane towards Stoke Canon to pass old cross at **Burrow Farm**. Carry straight on to pass **Oakhay Barton**. Note Stoke Canon level crossing on Exeter–Tiverton line ahead.

❼ Just before level crossing follow footpath sign **R** through kissing gate and along fenced path. Pass through another kissing gate and metal gate to join **dismantled railway** line. Pass through another kissing gate and go straight on. River Exe loops in on L; **Brampford Speke church** is ahead above river. Kissing gate leads over small bridge and into copse. Another kissing gate leads back into meadows (marshy in winter, but small wooden footbridge, **R**, can be used) and to footbridge over Exe.

❽ Once over bridge, retrace steps up path, turning **L** at lychgate; back through churchyard to car park.

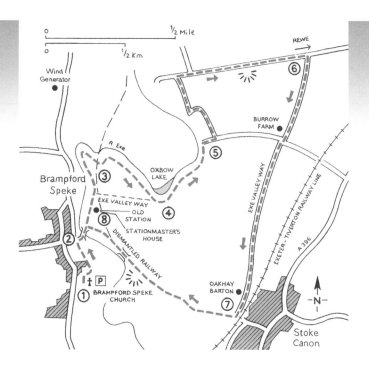

Steps Bridge A Dartmoor Outlier

5 miles (8km) 2hrs 45min **Ascent:** 393ft (120m)

Paths:	Woodland paths, open fields and country lanes, 7 stiles
Suggested map:	OS Explorer 110 Torquay & Dawlish
Grid reference:	SX 804883
Parking:	Free car park (and tourist information) at Steps Bridge

A climb up Heltor Rock and a church.

1 Cross road, following signs ('youth hostel'). Turn **R** up track, then **L**. At youth hostel, turn **R**, following signs ('**Heltor Farm**'). Path leads uphill through woodland. At T-junction turn **L** and over steps by gate into field.

2 Follow footpath posts up field. Go through gate and between gateposts (**Heltor Rock** to L). Pass signs ('**Lower Heltor Farm**') at gate to green lane; turn **L**.

3 Follow footpath signs **L** then **R** round farmhouse to track. Turn **L** up farm drive.

4 At top turn **L** ('Bridford'). Soon turn **L** over stile up narrow path to **Heltor**. Retrace steps to road; turn **L**.

5 Lane bends L, then R, to edge of **Bridford**. Turn **R** down lane ('Parish Hall & Church'). Follow path round churchyard, down steps and **R** to **Bridford Inn**.

6 Turn **L** from pub; follow lane through village. Take 3rd lane (Neadon Lane) on **R**, by telephone box. Past where bridleway joins (L) lane dips R, downhill; take **L**

fork ahead passing **Westbirch Farm** (R). Turn **L** at track to Birch Down Farm. Cross 2 stiles by barn; cross field, keeping wire fence (R). Cross stile and up R-H edge of next field to stile in top corner; cross wall and straight on through gorse bushes, towards footpath signpost. Cross stile by trees.

7 Continue along top of field, through 2 gates and down lane to **Lower Lowton Farm**. Turn **R** to footpath signpost; follow bridleway **R** ('**Woodlands**'). Keep to bridleway past barn (L); turn **R** through gate and downhill on lane. Cross track between fields via 2 gates, then through gate. Continue down banked lane to surfaced lane.

8 Turn **L** through middle gate ('Byway to **Steps Bridge**'). At edge of **Bridford Wood** (by National Trust sign) turn **R** following footpath signposts. Go **L**, then **R**; cross sandy track, keeping downhill. Path runs to **L**, high above river to **Steps Bridge**, to road opposite café. Turn **L** to return to car park.

Lustleigh Wooded Bovey Valley

5 miles (8km) 3hrs **Ascent:** 754ft (230m)

Paths: Steep rocky ascents/descents, rough paths and woodland

Suggested map: OS Outdoor Leisure 28 Dartmoor

Grid reference: SX 774815

Parking: By side of lane at Hammerslake

Exploring wooded Bovey Valley.

❶ With Lustleigh behind, walk ahead from car; turn **L** up path between houses 'Loganstones' and '**Grove**', following bridleway signs ('Cleave for **Water**'). At gate go ahead ('**Hunter's Tor**'); climb to top.

❷ Turn **R** through woodland; vegetation clears then follow path straight on over highest part of ridge and across remains of **Iron Age fort** to **Hunter's Tor**.

❸ Through gate **R** of tor; follow signed path **R** to another signed path **L**. Follow track downhill through gate; immediately **R** through another and downhill towards **Peck Farm**. Go through gate and down drive.

❹ Shortly after turn **L** through gate ('**Foxworthy Bridge**'); continue along wooded track. Pass through 2 gates to **Foxworthy**; turn **R**.

❺ Go **L** ('**Horsham**'). Follow track into woodland through gate. After 5 minutes follow signs **R** ('**Horsham** for Manaton & **Water**') to River Bovey. Follow river bank **L** to crossing (on boulders) at

Horsham Steps. If concerned about crossing river here, don't turn **L** for '**Horsham**' at Point **❺**, go **R** down drive, which crosses river. Take 1st footpath **L** and follow river to rejoin main route at Point **❻**.

❻ Cross, carefully; enter **nature reserve**. Follow path uphill through woodland and over stile. Keep **L** at 2 junctions; pass through gate by 2 cottages (note tree-branch porch) following signs ('**Water**') through **Letchole Plantation**.

❼ At crossroads of tracks turn **R** ('Manaton direct') to lane by cottages at **Water**. Take 2nd lane **R** to Kes Tor Inn.

❽ Retrace steps to crossroads. Go downhill to split in track. Keep **L** through gate; continue down path ('**Clam Bridge** for **Lustleigh Cleave**'). Cross river on split-log bridge; go uphill to signpost **L** ('Lustleigh via **Hammerslake**'). Go **L** and **L** again at next signpost (steep). Pass boulder; follow signs for **Hammerslake**. At gate turn **R** down path back to lane at start.

Bovey Tracey Dartmoor's National Park

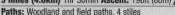

3 miles (4.8km) 1hr 30min **Ascent:** 196ft (60m) ⚠
Paths: Woodland and field paths, 4 stiles
Suggested map: OS Explorer 110 Torquay & Dawlish
Grid reference: SX 814782
Parking: Car park on the B3344 at lower end of Fore Street, Bovey Tracey, with tourist information office

Woodlands and an old railway line.

❶ Cross road; turn **R**, following signs ('Town centre shops'). Before bridge turn **L** along concrete walkway into Mill Marsh Park, past children's playground and through arboretum, past sports field to busy **A382** at **Hole Bridge** via kissing gate. Cross road carefully.

❷ Go through kissing gate; turn **R** to enter National Trust's **Parke Estate** on dismantled railway line. Follow path over river.

❸ Turn immediately **L** down wooden steps and over stile to follow river (L). Cross stile at end of field; continue through wooded strip, down steps and over footbridge and stile into next field.

❹ Signs point L for **Parke** and R for 'Railway Walk'; go straight on following **Riverside Walk** through field into woodland, then on raised walkway to river. Path winds on, then runs between woods with fields (R), then over footbridge to meet river at weir. Follow bank, ignoring broad track R. Two kissing gates lead out of

National Trust land and past footbridge (L). Shortly footpath turns **R** to cross railway track. Turn **L** and straight on to lane via kissing gate.

❺ Turn **L** ('Manaton'); pass between old railway bridge piers. Walk across **Wilsford Bridge**, ignoring signs ('Lustleigh') R. Continue up lane past **Forder gatehouses**, then uphill until lane bends **R**.

❻ Turn **L** over stile; re-enter **Parke Estate**. Wooded path is narrow. Go through wood and kissing gate to large field. Keep to **R** edge, heading downhill, to leave via kissing gate and down wooded path parallel to road.

❼ Path ends at kissing gate; turn **L** to cross parkland and driveway to **Parke** car park. Walk downhill to cross lower drive, then **L** to walk below house, ending at 5-bar gate. Turn **R** ('Riverside Walk') to cross river at **Parke Bridge**; keep ahead to join old railway track.

❽ Turn **R**; follow track until it crosses River Bovey to meet **A382**. Cross road to enter Mill Marsh Park and retrace steps to car.

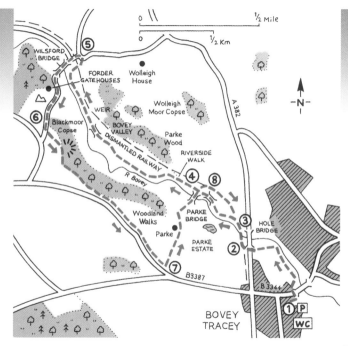

Dartington A Medieval Mansion

5 miles (8km) 2hrs 30min **Ascent:** 164ft (50m)

Paths: Fields, woodland tracks and country lanes, 4 stiles

Suggested map: OS Explorer 110 Torquay & Dawlish

Grid reference: SX 799628

Parking: Opposite entrance to Dartington Hall

Note: Larger organised groups should seek permission from the Property Administrator (01803 847000) at least 10 days in advance. All paths on Dartington Hall Estate are permissive unless otherwise marked

Around the Dartington Hall Estate.

1 From car park turn **L** downhill. Follow pavement to River Dart.

2 Turn **L** over stile and follow river northwards (can be very muddy after rain). Pass over stile, through strip of woodland and over another stile into meadow. At end cross stile to wooded track.

3 Walk along river edge of next field (**Park Copse** to L). At end of field cross stile into **Staverton Ford Plantation**. Where track veers **L** go through gate in wall ahead, then **R** to follow wooded path back towards river. Keep on path as it runs parallel with river, becoming broad woodland track through **North Wood**. When you see buildings through trees on R, leave track and walk downhill to metal gate and lane.

4 Turn **R** to cross **Staverton Bridge**. At level crossing turn **R** to pass through **Staverton Station**

yard into park-like area between railway and river. Follow path across single-track railway and walk on to lane by Sweet William Cottage.

5 Turn **R** and follow lane to end. Go ahead on small path to pass **Church of St Paul de Leon** (9th-century travelling preacher). Turn **L** at lane to pass public toilets, and **L** at junction to **Sea Trout Inn**. After break retrace steps to metal gate past **Staverton Bridge**.

6 Turn immediately **R** to rejoin track. Follow until it runs downhill and bends **L**. Walk towards gate on **R**. Turn **L** on narrow concrete path. Keep on concrete path, which leaves woodland and runs between wire fences to concrete drive at **Dartington Crafts Education Centre**. Follow drive to road.

7 Turn **L** to pass **Old Parsonage Farm**. Keep on road back to **Dartington Hall**, passing gardens and ruins of original church (R), until car park on **L**.

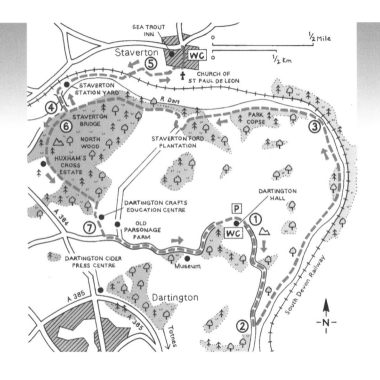

Coleton Fishacre Wartime Secrets

4½ miles (7.2km) 3hrs **Ascent:** 525ft (160m) ▲
Paths: Varying coast path, tracks and lanes, steep steps, 9 stiles
Suggested map: OS Outdoor Leisure 20 South Devon
Grid reference: SX 910513
Parking: National Trust car park at Coleton Camp

The delights of Coleton Fishacre.

❶ At car park, turn **R**; park along **R** edge. Through kissing gate in top **R** corner to take path towards gate and stile ('National Trust Coleton Barton Farm'). Go along field edge and over stile down to another stile at bottom of field, then **L** diagonally to another stile. Walk uphill to coast path (signs to **Pudcombe Cove** R).

❷ Turn **R**; follow path along cliff. Cross stile, walk steeply downhill and over footbridge to gate at bottom of **Coleton Fishacre** gardens (no public right of way into gardens here).

❸ Turn **L**, following coast path signs; pass steps to cove and go up steps; leave estate over stile and on to Coleton Cliffs. At next stile, path drops, then climbs above **Old Mill Bay**, followed by steep climb to **Outer Froward Point**. Path undulates, then climbs to back of **Froward Cove**.

❹ Turn **L**, following signs ('Kingswear') and ('Brownstone car park'). Cross stile; walk uphill; cross another stile. Take next coast path sign **L**, downhill through wooded section. Path undulates towards sea.

❺ Lookout at **Inner Froward Point** is next landmark, followed by 104 steps up cliff. Follow tramway uphill; keep to walkway and steps to pass disused wartime buildings. At top is junction of paths and wooden footpath sign.

❻ Turn **L** for Kingswear; walk through woodland behind Newfoundland Cove, over stile and down broad woodland track (estuary L). Go down 84 steps to **Mill Bay Cove**; turn **R** down tarmac way. Turn **L** over stile and climb 89 steps to lane, then 63 to another lane.

❼ Turn **R** ('Brownstone'). Shortly lane forks; take **R** fork downhill ('Access only to The Grange') to **Home Cottage**.

❽ Follow footpath signs **R** up path to concrete lane and on to pass **Higher Brownstone Farm**. Walk up lane passing National Trust car park, then gates to **Coleton Fishacre**, and back to car park.

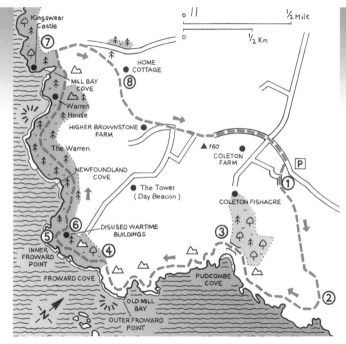

Dartmouth A Port and a Castle

3 miles (4.8km) 2hrs **Ascent:** 115ft (35m)
Paths: Easy coastal footpath and green lanes
Suggested map: OS Outdoor Leisure 20 South Devon
Grid reference: SX 874491
Parking: National Trust car parks at Little Dartmouth

Along the cliffs to Dartmouth Castle.

❶ Car parks at **Little Dartmouth** are signposted off B3205 (from A379 Dartmouth-to-Stoke Fleming road). Go through **R-H** car park, following signs ('Coast Path Dartmouth'). Continue through kissing gate, keeping hedge R. Walk through next field, then kissing gate to coast path.

❷ Turn **L** (lovely views west to start and east towards Day Beacon above Kingswear). Coast path runs inland from cliff edge, but go ahead to walk above Warren Point.

❸ Continue **L** to pass above **Western Combe Cove** (steps down to sea) then **Combe Point** (take care; long drop to sea from here).

❹ Rejoin coast path through open gateway in wall; follow above **Shinglehill Cove**. Path turns inland, passes through gate, becomes narrow and overgrown, and twists along back of **Willow Cove**. It passes through wooded section (with field on L), then

climbs around back of **Compass Cove**. Keep going to pass through gate. Keep **L** to reach wooden footpath post, then turn sharp **R**, down valley to cliff edge. Follow path on, through gate near **Blackstone Point**.

❺ Leave path **R** to clamber down on to rocks here (superb view over mouth of estuary). Retrace steps and continue on coast path as it turns inland along side of estuary and runs through deciduous woodland.

❻ Path meets surfaced lane opposite **Compass Cottage**; go **R** on to lane and immediately **R** again steeply downhill, keeping wall to L. At turning space go **R** down steps to **castle** and **café**.

❼ Retrace your route up steps to tarmac lane at Point ❻, then **L** to pass **Compass Cottage**, and straight on up steep lane ('**Little Dartmouth**') and through kissing gate on to National Trust land.

❽ Path runs along top of field and through 5-bar gate on to green lane. Go through gate and farmyard at **Little Dartmouth**; continue on lane to car park.

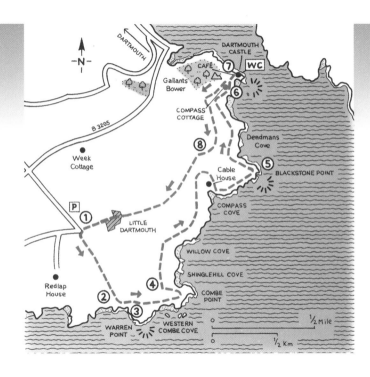

East Prawle The Deep South

4 miles (6.4km) 2hrs **Ascent:** 394ft (120m) ▲3

Paths: Green lanes, fields and coast path, rocky in places, 3 stiles
Suggested map: OS Outdoor Leisure 20 South Devon
Grid reference: SX 781365
Parking: Around green in East Prawle (honesty box contributions)

A land of shipwrecks and smugglers, gannets and skuas.

1 Walk down lane towards sea, leaving green (L) and phone box on R, following footpath ('Prawle Point'). Shortly lane turns L; go ahead along rutted green lane ('Public Bridleway Gammon Head').

2 Green lane ends at T-junction (metal gate opposite); turn **L** down narrow grassy path between old walls (views ahead). Follow path to footpath post.

3 Turn **R** and immediately downhill to coast path high above secluded **Maceley Cove**, with Gammon Head R. Turn **L** and walk along path above **Elender Cove** (steep access to both beaches but take care).

4 Path leads through kissing gate and on around **Signalhouse Point**. Steep ascent rewarded with fine views ahead to wreck of Demetrios on rocks, with Prawle Point beyond. Follow footpath posts through kissing gate and across grassy down, keeping to **R** of **coastguard lookout** ahead.

5 At **coastguard lookout** enjoy superb views east to Lannacombe, Mattiscombe Sand and start. Take time to explore visitor centre (excellent details about area). To continue, follow grassy path inland towards old coastguard cottages.

6 Turn **R** through gate to pass in front of cottages and along edge of level, grassy wavecut platform which lies below original Pleistocene cliffs here. Pass through kissing gate and along level meadows above low cliffs. Go through next kissing gate, past next footpath post and over ivy-covered stile. Pass around edge of next field (Maelcombe House now ahead).

7 Follow path as it turns inland and, shortly, cross stone wall. Turn immediately **L** up edge of field. At end of hedge go **L** up track.

8 Take 1st stile **R** to go up field (wonderful views back to coast). Cross stone stile at top and continue **R** up narrow rocky track to join lane, ascending **R** steeply back to village.

35 East Portlemouth The Kingsbridge Estuary

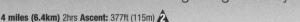

4 miles (6.4km) 2hrs **Ascent:** 377ft (115m)
Paths: Good coast path, field paths and tracks
Suggested map: OS Outdoor Leisure 20 South Devon
Grid reference: SX 746385
Parking: Near phone box in East Portlemouth or in small parking bay

A stroll around sleepy East Portlemouth.

1 Park on verge near phone box at **East Portlemouth** (or parking area – contributions to village hall fund). Walk through parking area and downhill on narrow tarmac footpath ('Salcombe'), which leads to steps.

2 Reach lane at bottom; turn **R** to visit **Venus Café** or to catch ferry to **Salcombe**. To continue with walk, turn **L** along lane as it follows edge of estuary (official route of coast path, passing exclusive residences in almost sub-tropical surroundings).

3 Lane leads to beach at **Mill Bay**. Follow coast path signs for Gara Rock along edge of wood (lovely views across estuary, and glimpses of little coves).

4 At **Limebury Point** reach open cliff. From here there are great views to South Sands and Overbecks opposite and craggy Bolt Head. Coast path veers eastwards below **Portlemouth Down**.

5 Path undulates steeply (rocky in places). Keep going until bench and viewpoint over beach at Rickham Sands. Just beyond, as coast path continues R along cliffs (reasonable access to beach), take **L** fork and climb up below lookout to reach wall in front of **Gara Rock Hotel**.

6 Turn **L** to hotel drive; walk straight on up lane. Shortly turn **L** through gate in hedge ('Mill Bay'). Walk across field (roped-off area indicates car park for beach) with views to **Salcombe** and Malborough church beyond. Go through small copse, then gate and across farm track. Go through metal gate down public footpath.

7 This leads on to beautiful bridlepath, running downhill beneath pollarded lime trees (grassy combe to R). Path leads past car park to **Mill Bay**.

8 Turn **R** along lane. To avoid steps, watch for footpath sign pointing **R**, up path to regain **East Portlemouth** and your car; if not, continue along lane and retrace steps up steep tarmac path.

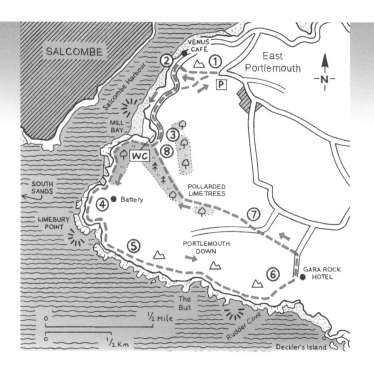

Kingston Peace and Solitude

5½ miles (8.8km) 2hrs 30min **Ascent:** 394ft (120m)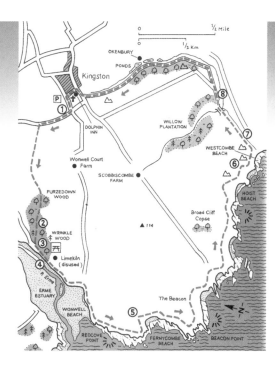

Paths: Fields, tracks and good coast path, 7 stiles

Suggested map: OS Outdoor Leisure 20 South Devon

Grid reference: SX 635478

Parking: By the church in Kingston village

A magical part of the county's south coast that is seldom visited.

❶ With church L, follow lane uphill to Wonwell Gate and turn **R** down lane ('Wonwell Beach'). When it bends L then R, turn **L** through gate/stile and straight on, keeping hedge L. Pass through hedge into next field; follow sign **R**, diagonally across field to enter **Furzedown Wood** over stile into green lane.

❷ This leads into next field; cross, then go over stile into **Wrinkle Wood** and follow path downhill to lane.

❸ Turn **L**; limited parking for beach here. Walk down to **Erme estuary** (attractive spot for picnic).

❹ Retrace steps and follow coast path signs up steps **R** ('Bigbury'). Follow wooded path, which leads on to and along back of **Wonwell Beach**. Go up steps, over stile and straight on along estuary to **Redcove Point** (superb views to Battisborough Island opposite).

❺ Path veers eastwards over stile (National Trust Scobbiscombe Farm), then sweeps across broad grassy area above **Fernycombe Beach** to **Beacon Point** (glorious views ahead). Walk through small gate, into combe and up to gate. Pause at bench overlooking **Hoist Beach**, before path drops down into combe and climbs up through another gate.

❻ Follow steep (often slippery) descent to Westcombe Beach. Take great care here, parts are stepped (steps sandy and it's easy to skid).

❼ Turn **L** over stile at back of beach, following signs for **Kingston** (permissive path, unmarked on maps). Path has wire fence (L) and stream (R); walk over wooden footbridge (**R**) to cross stream and enter willow plantation. Path twists out through strip of woodland.

❽ Cross stile and go straight on up, gradually ascending green lane (bridleway to **Kingston**). Continue on to pass ponds at **Okenbury** R (muddy in places). Track runs into tarmac lane, and back uphill into **Kingston**. Turn **R**, then **L** to church and car.

Bigbury-on-Sea Burgh Island Paradise

3 miles (4.8km) 1hr 45min **Ascent:** 246ft (75m) ▲

Paths: Fields, tracks (muddy in winter) and coast path, 4 stiles

Suggested map: OS Outdoor Leisure 20 South Devon

Grid reference: SX 651442

Parking: Huge car park at Bigbury-on-Sea

An Art Deco dream and Devon's oldest inn.

❶ Leave car park through entrance. Follow coast path signs **R**, **L** towards road, then **L** again up grassy area. Turn **L** before bungalow, then **L** (unmarked path) to road. Turn **R** and walk steeply uphill to **Mount Folly Farm**.

❷ Turn **L** along track ('Ringmore'). At top of field is junction of paths; go through gate **L**, then through gate ahead, keeping downhill. Cross stile; walk downhill through kissing gate. Cross farm track and up field to stile, then descend steps into narrow lane.

❸ Cross over, following signs ('Ringmore'), through **L** of 2 gates. Walk down into next combe, keeping hedgebank **R**. Cross stream at bottom on concrete walkway, and over stile. Ignore path **L**; go ahead, uphill, through plantation and gate on to path between fence and hedge.

❹ Pass through kissing gate; turn **R** through open gateway. Turn **L** uphill to metal gate/stile to join track leading to **Ringmore**. Turn **R** at lane, then **L** at church to Journey's End (**R**).

❺ From pub turn **R** down narrow lane which gives way to footpath, which winds round to tarmac lane. Turn **L** downhill. Walk on down track ('**Lower Manor Farm**'); keep going down past 'National Trust **Ayrmer Cove**' notice. After small gate track splits; keep **L** (unsigned) and straight on.

❻ Turn **L** through kissing gate; walk towards cove on path above combe (**L**). Pass through gate and over 2 stiles to beach.

❼ Follow coast path ('**Challaborough**') **L** over footbridge then climb steeply uphill to cliff top (views over **Burgh Island**). Cliffs crumbly here – take care. Path is narrow, with wire fence **L**, leading to Challaborough (holiday camp).

❽ Turn **R** along beach road and follow track leading uphill along coast towards Bigbury. Go straight on to tarmac road, then **R** on gravel path to car park.

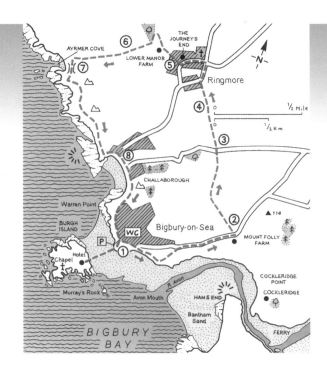

Cadover Bridge Mysteries of the Dewerstone

3½ miles (5.7km) 1hr 45min Ascent: 180ft (55m)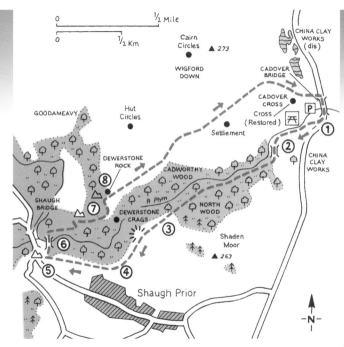

Paths: Woodland paths, some rocky, and rough moorland, 4 stiles
Suggested map: OS Outdoor Leisure 28 Dartmoor
Grid reference: SX 555646
Parking: Free car park at Cadover Bridge

Industrial archaeology and a hard climb past the eerie Dewerstone Crags.

1 From car park, walk away from **Cadover Bridge**, (river on R). Cross stile into willow plantation.

2 Wooden ladder down bank leads to short stretch of pasture. Stile and footbridge lead into **North Wood** oak woodland. Choice of route here; keep to path with large pipe set in ground.

3 Leave **North Wood** over stile and follow path through open brackeny area; **River Plym** below on R. (Note group of **Dewerstone Crags** ahead on other side of valley.) Path leads into mixed silver birch and oak past ruined building, then forks. Take **R** fork slightly downhill to track and gate.

4 Turn **R** inside wire fence, following footpath sign ('**Shaugh Bridge**'). Stay within woods as path twists downhill. Path leads over stile past notice ('Hazardous Area: Proceed with Caution') – can be slippery. Pass settling tank (R); path ends at road.

5 Turn immediately **R**; take **L** fork then down steps into Shaugh Bridge car park. Turn **R**; walk through car park towards river.

6 Cross river via railed wooden footbridge; enter **Goodameavy** (National Trust). Follow path **R**. It becomes rocky track leading above river and winds steeply uphill. Where path goes straight ahead and there is sharp bend R, keep **R** and uphill until you see top of **Dewerstone Crags** through trees R.

7 Path becomes rocky scramble **L** and up to leave woods and on to moorland to **Dewerstone Rock**.

8 Turn 90 degrees **R** at rock; follow grassy path along ridge passing Oxen Tor and over **Wigford Down**, keeping **Cadworthy Wood** and Plym Valley R. Keep straight on to boundary wall of wood, then **L** to follow wall around fields. Eventually wall veers R; walk downhill past **Cadover Cross** (views of china clay works beyond). Head towards bridge, cross over on road and walk back to car.

Meldon Reservoir Dartmoor's Highest Tors

4¼ miles (6.8km) 2hrs 45min Ascent: 722ft (220m)

Paths: Grassy tracks and open moorland

Suggested map: OS Outdoor Leisure 28 Dartmoor

Grid reference: SX 563917

Parking: Car park at Meldon Reservoir (voluntary contributions)

An ancient oak woodland and views of Yes Tor and High Willhays.

❶ Walk up stone steps by toilets, through gate and **L** on tarmac way towards dam, ('Bridleway to Moor'). Cross dam.

❷ Turn **R** along track. Stile (R) leads to waterside picnic area. Don't cross stile, but leave track here to go straight on, following edge of reservoir through side valley and over footbridge. Narrow path undulates to steepish descent at end of reservoir to meet broad marshy valley of West Okement River; **Corn Ridge** 1,762ft (537m) lies ahead.

❸ Cross footbridge; take path along **L** edge of valley, keeping to bottom of slope on **L**. Path broadens uphill and becomes grassy as it rounds **Vellake Corner** above river below **R**.

❹ At top of hill, track levels; you can glimpse **Black Tor Copse** ahead. Follow river upstream past waterfall and weir, **R** of granite enclosure, and along **L** bank through open moorland to enter **Black Tor Copse**.

❺ Retrace steps out of trees and veer **R** around copse edge, uphill aiming for **L** outcrop of **Black Tor** on ridge above. Walk through bracken to tor; no definite path here, but it's straightforward. Outcrop on **R** rises to 1,647ft (502m).

❻ Return to grassy area north of tor. Turn **R** to continue away from river valley behind, aiming for track visible ahead over **Longstone Hill**. To find track go slightly downhill from tor to small stream. Turn **L**, then **R** towards 3 granite blocks marking track.

❼ Intermittent track runs straight across open moor (good views of quarry ahead). Where **Red-a-Ven Brook** Valley appears below **R**, enjoy view of Row Tor, West Mill Tor and Yes Tor. High Willhays, Dartmoor's highest tor, lies just out of sight to **R**. Track veers **L** around end of hill and drops back to reservoir.

❽ Turn **R** to rejoin track back over dam and back to car park.

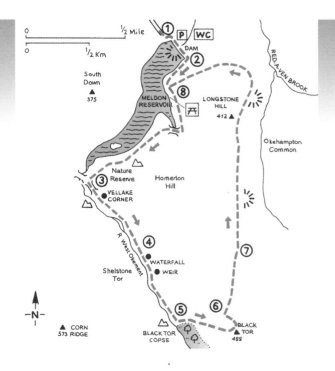

Clovelly Without the Crowds

5 miles (8km) 2hrs 15min **Ascent:** 410ft (125m) ⚠️3

Paths: Grassy coast path, woodland and farm tracks, 4 stiles

Suggested map: OS Explorer 126 Clovelly & Hartland

Grid reference: SS 285259

Parking: National Trust car park at Brownsham

Pheasants and follies – and a different way into Clovelly.

❶ Leave car park over stile opposite entrance. Walk along field and through gate into woods. Follow signs ('Footpath to coast path') to pass bench. Keep ahead ('Mouth Mill & coast path'). Cross stile to coast path.

❷ Go **R** over stile into field on **Brownsham Cliff**. Keep to L edge, across stile, down steps and L round next field. Cross stile; go downhill through woodland. Leave trees; turn **L** towards sea at **Mouth Mill**.

❸ Follow coast path across stream by stepping stones. Clamber up rocky gully **L** and turn **R** on to track, on bend. Keep going **L**, uphill.

❹ Shortly follow coast path signs **L**, then immediately **R**. Go **L** up steps to follow path uphill towards cliffs below **Gallantry Bower**.

❺ Follow signed path through woodland to pass folly ('Angel's Wings'). Where path leads straight on to church, keep **L** following signs and via gate through

edge of **Clovelly Court estate** (R). Pass into woods via kissing gate. Path winds down and up past shelter, then through kissing gate into field. Keep to **L**; continue through gate and oak trees to road at gate. Follow coast path signs on to road leading to top of **Clovelly** village below **Visitor Centre**.

❻ Walk up **Wrinkleberry Lane** (R of Hobby Drive ahead) to lane, past school and on to road. Turn **R**; where road bends R go through gates to **Clovelly Court**. At T-junction follow bridleway signs **L** ('**Court Farm** & sawmills') through farm, metal gate (sometimes open) and along track. Pass through small wooded section and walk on to hedge at end of field.

❼ Turn **R**, then **L** through gate (by footpath sign). At bottom of field go through gate into plantation, downhill.

❽ Turn **L** at forest track, following bridleway signs. Turn **R** up track to Lower Brownsham Farm. Turn **L** for car park.

Wimbleball Lake Woodland Water

6 miles (9.7km) 3hrs **Ascent:** 750ft (230m) ⓷
Paths: Rough descent, long climb, easy track between, 1 stile
Suggested map: OS Outdoor Leisure 9 Exmoor
Grid reference: SS 969285
Parking: Frogwell Lodge car park, Haddon Hill

Natural and artificial landscapes merge on this route through wooded valley, heath and across the Wimbleball Dam.

❶ Leave car park by small gate **L** of toilets. Turn **R** to cross tarred track; head downhill on small path running through gorse, grass and heather until open birch woods give rise to easier going. If you lose path keep going downhill. Above reservoir is stony track.

❷ Turn **L**. Track emerges on to open grassland and starts rising to L. Look for stile down on **R**, into woodland. Cross; turn **L** on path that emerges near **Wimbleball Dam**. Side-trip to dam gives fine views of **Hartford Bottom** below.

❸ Return along dam and turn **R** into tarmac lane ('Bury 2½'). At bottom keep ahead on concrete path ('Bridleway'). With bridge ahead, bear **L** on to grass track ('Bridleway to Bury') which leads to ford; watch for footbridge on **R**. Cross then take track between houses; turn **L** into **Hartford**.

❹ Turn **L** ('Bury 2') on track, passing through woods beside **River Haddeo**. Track now stony to village of **Bury**.

❺ Turn **L** to packhorse bridge beside road's ford. Ignore riverside track on L; continue for 180yds (165m); turn **L** at bridleway sign. Pass between houses to sign for Haddon Hill, and sunken track which climbs steeply; stream at bottom flows over orange bedrock. At top track continues between hedges, before turning **L** for short climb to **Haddon Farm**.

❻ Pass to **L** of farm's buildings, on to access track. After ¼ mile (400m) reach corner of wood. Shortly stile above leads into wood. Ignore pointing signpost but bear **L** to go up L-H side of wood to gate on to open hill. Go up alongside wood to top corner.

❼ Take track bearing **L** to cross crest of hill. Turn **R**, on wide track running to top of **Haddon Hill**. Continue downhill to car park.

Horner Exmoor's Red Deer

4½ miles (7.2km) 2hrs 30min **Ascent:** 1,000ft (300m) ▲

Paths: Broad paths, with some stonier ones, steep in places, no stiles

Suggested map: OS Outdoor Leisure 9 Exmoor

Grid reference: SS 898455

Parking: National Trust car park (free) at Horner

On the trail of Exmoor's red deer in the woodlands under Dunkery Beacon.

❶ Leave National Trust car park in Horner village past toilets; turn **R** to track leading into **Horner Wood**, crossing bridge and passing field before rejoining **Horner Water**. Take footpath alongside stream instead of track, leading to same place. Ignore 1st footbridge; continue along track to where sign, ('Dunkery Beacon') points **L** towards 2nd footbridge.

❷ Ignore footbridge. Keep on track, then fork **L** on path alongside **West Water**. This rejoins track; after ½ mile (800m) bridleway sign points back to R. Look down to **L** for footbridge.

❸ Cross on to path that slants up to **R**. After 200yds (183m) turn **L** on to smaller path that turns uphill alongside **Prickslade Combe**. Path reaches little stream at cross-path, with wood top visible above. Turn **L**, across stream, on path contouring through top of wood, which emerges into open to tree with bench

and fine view over top of woodlands to Porlock Bay.

❹ Continue ahead on grassy track, with car park of **Webber's Post** visible ahead. Deep valley of **East Water** lies ahead. Turn down **L** on path back into birchwoods, to meet larger track in valley bottom.

❺ Turn downstream, crossing footbridge over East Water, beside ford. Shortly bear **R** on to ascending path. At top of steep section turn **R** on sunken path climbing to Webber's Post car park.

❻ Walk to **L**, round car park, to path ('Permitted Bridleway') to Horner. (Do not take pink-surfaced, easy-access path immediately to R.) After 80yds (73m) bear **L** on to wider footpath. Keep ahead down wide, gentle spur, with deep valley of **Horner Water** on L. As spur steepens, footpath meets crossing track ('Windsor Path').

❼ Turn **R** for about 30 paces, then take descending path ('Horner'). Path widens and finally meets wide track with wooden steps; turn **L** into Horner.

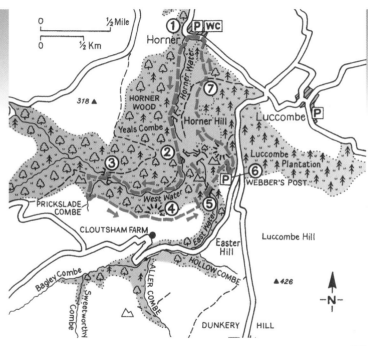

Lype Hill To Brendon's Heights

5¾ miles (9.2km) 3hrs **Ascent:** 850ft (260m)

Paths: A rugged track, then little-used field bridleways, 4 stiles

Suggested map: OS Outdoor Leisure 9 Exmoor

Grid reference: SS 923387

Parking: Village car park (free) on A396 at Wheddon Cross

A sunken lane from Wheddon Cross leads up to Lype Hill, the high point of the Brendons.

❶ From main crossroads head towards Dunster; bear **R** at war memorial to pass car park on R-H side. After school, bear **R**, following signpost to Puriton (Popery Lane). Sunken lane runs to **Cutcombe Cross**; keep ahead ('Luxborough via **Putham Ford**') then bear **L** at sign into Putham Lane.

❷ Horses and tractors use track. At bottom it crosses ford, with footbridge alongside. Keep ahead on to lane heading uphill.

❸ At top, field gate on **R** has inconspicuous footpath signpost, leading on to green track that runs below, then into wood. Look for footpath sign and stile beside stream below. Cross water and take path on **R**, into open space. Slightly wider path above slants up along bracken clearing. After stile it follows foot of wood, to join forest road, then tarred lane.

❹ Turn **L**, down wide verge; take upper of 2 gates on **R**, with stile and footpath sign. Head up side of wooded combe and across top. Sea view on **L**, stile and gate ahead. Don't cross; turn **R**, and **R** again across top of field by trig point on **Lype Hill** and views of Dunkery Beacon, Wales and Dartmoor.

❺ Through gate keep ahead across field, with tumulus 70yds (64m) on L; after gate bear **L**, following fence on L to its corner. Gate ahead leads on to road. Cross to signposted gate; bear **L** to field's far corner. Turn **L** alongside beech bank to waymarked gate. Turn **R**, with fence on R, and head down along field edges towards **Pitleigh Farm**. Gate in deer fencing leads on to driveway **L** of farm.

❻ Cross driveway on to green track. This becomes fenced-in field edge to deer-fence gate on L. Turn **R** to continue as before with hedges now on R. After 2 fields reach hedged track. This runs down to crossroads in Popery Lane.

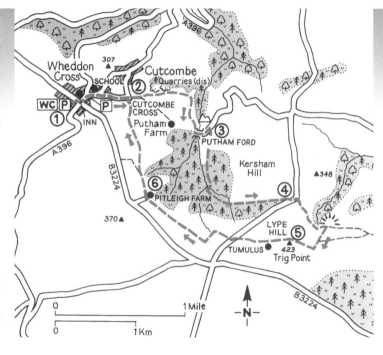

Kilve Along the Quantock Coastline

3 miles (4.8km) 1hr 30min **Ascent:** 250ft (80m)
Paths: Tracks, field paths, and grassy cliff top, 7 stiles
Suggested map: OS Explorer 140 Quantock Hills & Bridgwater
Grid reference: ST 144442
Parking: Pay-and-display at sea end of Sea Lane

A stimulating walk including Tudor villages, breezy cliffs, industrial remnants and geology underfoot.

1 From car park head back along lane to **ruined chantry**. Turn into churchyard through lychgate. Pass to **L** of church, to kissing gate.

2 Signposted track crosses field to gate with stile; bear **R** to another gate with stile and pass along foot of **East Wood**. (At far end, stile allows wandering into wood, April to August only.) Ignoring stile on **L**, keep ahead to field gate with stile and track crossing stream.

3 Track bends **L** past gardens and ponds of **East Quantoxhead**. Turn **R**, towards Tudor **Court House**, but before gateway bear **L** into car park. Pass through to tarred path beyond 2 kissing gates. In open field path bears **R**, to **St Mary's Church**.

4 Return to 1st kissing gate but don't go through; instead bear **R** to field gate, and cross field beyond to lane. Turn **R** and, where lane bends **L**, keep ahead on to green track. At top, turn **R** at 'Permissive path' notice-board.

5 Follow field edges down to cliff top, and turn **R**. Clifftop path leads to stile before sharp dip, with ruined **limekiln** opposite, built around 1770 to process limestone from Wales. Most of rest of Somerset is limestone, but it was easier to bring it by sea across Bristol Channel.

6 Turn round head of dip, and back **L** to cliff top. Here iron ladder descends to foreshore: you can see alternating layers of blue-grey lias (type of limestone) and grey shale. Fossils can be found here, but note that cliffs are unstable – hard hats are now standard wear for geologists. Alternatively, given suitably trained dog and right sort of spear, you could pursue traditional sport of 'glatting' – hunting conger eels in rock pools. Continue along wide clifftop path until tarred path bears **R**, crossing stream into car park.

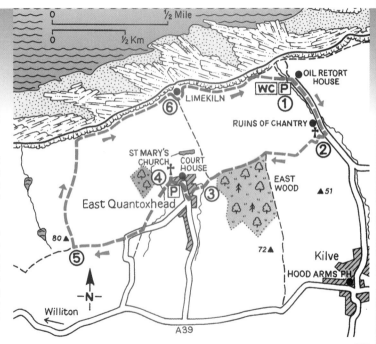

Holford A Quantock Amble

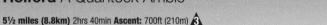

5½ miles (8.8km) 2hrs 40min **Ascent:** 700ft (210m) ⚠️

Paths: Wide, smooth paths, with one slightly rough descent, no stiles

Suggested map: OS Explorer 140 Quantock Hills & Bridgwater

Grid reference: ST 154410

Parking: At back of Holford (free)

A ramble in the Quantocks in the footsteps of Wordsworth and Coleridge.

❶ Two tracks leave road beside car park. Take **R-H** track, marked with bridleway sign, which becomes earth track through woods, with **Hodder's Combe Brook** on R. After ¾ mile (1.2km) track fords stream and forks. Take **R-H** option, entering side-valley. Path runs up valley floor, rising through oakwoods floored with bilberry ('whortleberry'), then mixed heather and bracken, to Quantock ridge. As ground eases, keep ahead over 2 cross-tracks to **Bicknoller Post**.

❷ To R (north) of col ridge divides: take **L-H** branch ('Beacon Hill'); pass to **L** side of marker stake on broad track. Keep ahead on widest track. Bear **L** to trig point on **Beacon Hill**.

❸ At trig point turn half-**R** to marker-post on main track. Smaller path descends ahead, into **Smith's Combe**. Weaving path crosses stream several times.

❹ At foot of valley, with green fields below, is 4-way

'Quantock Greenway' signpost: turn **R** (green arrow), uphill. Path runs around base of hills, with belt of trees below, then green fields. At 1st spur crest is another signpost, 3-way: keep ahead for Holford. Path drops to cross stream, **Dens Combe**. After ¼ mile (400m) it drops towards gate leading on to tarmac.

❺ Don't go through gate; strike uphill to another 'Quantock Greenway' signpost. Keep uphill (green arrow) to pass above pink house on to tarred lane. Take track ahead below several houses. Sign indicates Quantock Hills Youth Hostel down to L, but stay on lane; it runs out past Alfoxton, with walled garden of grand house (once poet William Wordsworth's, now hotel) on L and stable block on R. At foot of hotel driveway is parking area.

❻ Follow lane for 650yds (594m) then, as it bends R, look out for waymarker and railings down in trees. Below is footbridge leading across into Holford. Turn **R**; at 1st junction turn **R** again, to car park.

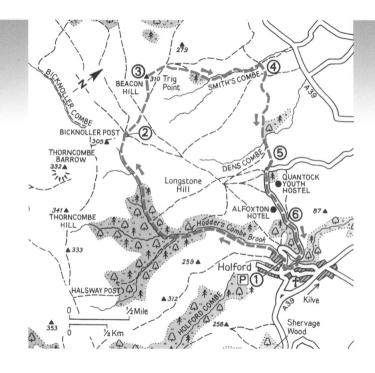

Wiveliscombe Wool Town and the Tone

6 miles (9.7km) 3hrs 15min **Ascent:** 1,000ft (300m)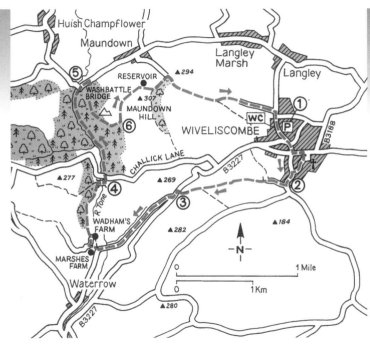

Paths: Tracks, a quiet lane, a few field edges, 1 stile
Suggested map: OS Explorer 128 Taunton & Blackdown Hills
Grid reference: ST 080279
Parking: North Street, Wiveliscombe

A pretty village and a wooded riverside on the edge of the Brendons.

❶ Turn **L** out of car park into Square; head down High Street and turn **L** at traffic lights (Church Street). Turn **R**, down steps under arch, to Rotton Row. Continue to South Street; turn **L** along pavement.

❷ At end of 30mph limit turn **R**, into lane; go ahead through gate with footpath sign. Cross stile ahead, and bottom edges of 2 fields. Stile in hedge ahead has grown over, so head up to **L** to gateway before returning to foot of field to reach farm buildings. Go up **L-H** edge of field above to gate on to **B3227**.

❸ Turn **L**, then **R** into lane heading downhill. After ¾ mile (1.2km) it crosses **River Tone** and bends L at **Marshes Farm**. Keep ahead, on track marked by broken bridleway sign. Do not turn R here into track towards **Wadham's Farm**; keep uphill to deeply sunken lane. Turn **R**, descending towards farm, but at 1st buildings turn **L** (track runs up River Tone). With

houses visible ahead, turn **R** at T-junction; cross footbridge and turn **L** to **Challick Lane**.

❹ Continuing track upstream is currently beside River Tone: polite enquiry at farm will let you through between buildings. Track continues upstream through pleasant woodland to **Washbattle Bridge**.

❺ Turn **R**, along road, for 200yds (183m). Signed forest road leads uphill on **R**. At highest point, with pheasant fence alongside, bear **L** on to wide path that continues uphill. At wood edge cross bottom corner of field to woodland opposite then turn uphill alongside to gate.

❻ Go through gate and turn **L**, with hedge beside it on L. Next gate opens on to hedged track which turns **R**, and passes **reservoir** at summit of **Maundown Hill**. At top of tarred public road turn **R** on to track that becomes descending, hedged path. At signposted fork turn **L** on to contouring path. Soon lane leads down into town, with car park near by on **R**.

Stapley Close to the Border

3 miles (4.8km) 1hr 40min **Ascent:** 500ft (150m)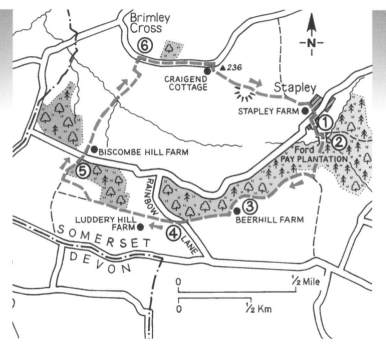

Paths: Field edges, small woodland paths, 8 stiles

Suggested map: OS Explorer 128 Taunton & Blackdown Hills

Grid reference: ST 188136

Parking: Small pull-in beside water treatment works at east end of Stapley; verge parking at walk start

Stapley's little valley looks down over the county boundary into Devon.

1 Phone box marks start of walk. Some 20 paces below it lane runs between houses. After 100yds (91m) keep ahead on to shady path. At stile bear **R** to ford with footbridge.

2 Head up wide track. At junction cross on to waymarked path, which heads uphill, following bank, to stile. In field beyond bear **R**, to field corner and stile back into woodland. Path runs along top edge of **Pay Plantation**, emerging near **Beerhill Farm**.

3 Bear **L** for 100yds (91m) to waymarked gate, and 2nd just beyond. Pass to **R** of cowshed to reach small pool. Pass **R** of pool, to gate; follow top edge of wood to **Rainbow Lane**.

4 Cross lane to signposted stile. Pass along **L** edge of long narrow field; over on **L**, **Luddery Hill Farm** is built of flinty-looking chert. Stile leads into ash wood. Path runs along top edge of wood. With isolated house

visible ahead, waymarker indicates diverted right of way bearing **R**. Path slants downhill, to meet driveway at bend. Cross on to wide path just above driveway. At end of wood turn down **R**, to rejoin driveway to road below.

5 Cross into trackway of **Biscombe Hill Farm**. Bear **L** to field gate, and go down **R** edge of field to muddy hedge gap on **R**. Slant down following field to stile at bottom **R-H** corner, with stepping stones across stream beyond. Go up **R-H** edge of next field to stile leading on to sunken track; turn **L** and follow it up to lane.

6 Turn **R**, up road. Where it levels and bends **L**, turn **R** into driveway of **Craigend Cottage**. Turn **L** along field tops, with hedge bank on your **L** and view of Devon over your **R** shoulder. After stile, field gate leads to tractor track. After short, muddy passage past **Stapley Farm** reach village road at phone box.

Blackdown Hills Prior's Park Woodlands

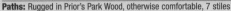

5 miles (8km) 2hrs 40min **Ascent:** 700ft (210m) **2**

Paths: Rugged in Prior's Park Wood, otherwise comfortable, 7 stiles

Suggested map: OS Explorer 128 Taunton & Blackdown Hills

Grid reference: ST 211182

Parking: Roadside pull-off between post office and White Lion, Blagdon Hill

Prior's Park Wood is at its best with autumn's colours or spring's bluebells.

1 Walk starts at phone box opposite White Lion, handsome 17th-century inn. Cross stile and follow **L** edge of triangular field to another stile into Curdleigh Lane. Cross into ascending **Quarry Lane**. Bend **L** between buildings of Quarry House, on to track running up into **Prior's Park Wood**.

2 From mid-April **Prior's Park Wood** is delightful with bluebells and other wild flowers. It is also fine (but possibly muddy) in late October and November. Where main track bends **L** and descends slightly, keep uphill on smaller one. This eventually declines into muddy trod, slanting up and leftwards to small gate at top of wood.

3 Pass along wood's top edge to gate. Red-and-white poles mark line across next field to another gate. After 50yds (46m) turn **R**, between buildings of **Prior's Park Farm**, to its access track and road. Turn **L** and

follow road with care (it's fairly fast section), towards **Holman Clavel Inn**.

4 Just before inn turn **L** into forest track. Where track ends small path runs ahead, zig-zagging down before crossing stream. At wood's edge turn **R** up wider path to **B3170**.

5 At once turn **L** on lane ('Feltham'). After ½ mile (800m), wide gateway on **L** leads to earth track. This runs along top of Adcombe Wood then down inside it, giving very pleasant descent.

6 Once below wood follow track downhill for 180yds (165m). Look for gate with signpost on **L-H** side. Go through it and follow hedge on **R** to stile and footbridge, then bend **L**, below foot of wood, to another stile. Ignore stile into wood on **L**, but continue along wood's foot to next field corner. Here further stile enters wood but turn **R**, beside hedge, to concrete track. Turn **L** – track becomes Curdleigh Lane, leading back into **Blagdon Hill**.

Ilminster A Walk in the Woods

5¾ miles (9.2km) 2hrs 40min **Ascent:** 500ft (150m)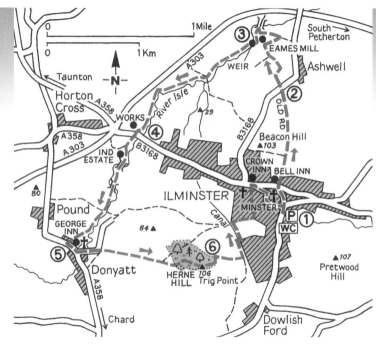

Paths: Tracks, wide paths, and riverside field edges, 12 stiles
Suggested map: OS Explorer 128 Taunton & Blackdown Hills
Grid reference: ST 362144
Parking: Pay-and-display in Ditton Street, signposted from nearby Market Cross

A pleasing riverside and woodland ramble.

❶ From car park aim for town centre and head uphill on North Street. With ancient **Bell Inn** on L, continue on path (Old Road), rising past beacon fire-basket and mobile phone mast before descending to **B3168**.

❷ Cross with care into hedged byway. Where it forks, keep **R**, to **Eames Mill**. Turn **R**, along waymarked access track. After 220yds (201m) concrete track turns back **L**. Just before bridge turn **L** over stile; follow **River Isle** upstream. Rights of way don't allow more straightforward route.

❸ Cross weir then head upstream with river to **L**. After 1 mile (1.6km) reach car park of Powrmatic works, and **B3168** beyond.

❹ Cross on to track ('Industrial Estate'). Pass along river bank to **L** of buildings, then between piles of ironwork to footbridge. With river on **R**, head upstream on fenced way to re-cross on another footbridge. Continue over stiles along **R-H** bank. With tower of **Donyatt church** ahead, cross diagonally **R** to gate on to road.

❺ Turn **L** through village, and bear **L** past church. Head straight up **Herne Hill** as lane becomes track, then field-edge path, then earth path through Herne Hill Wood, whose summit is under tall beeches. Wide avenue ahead leads to field corner. Continue inside wood, passing bench and trig point on **R**, and going down to wood's foot. Turn back **L** for 90yds (82m) to gate on **R**.

❻ Wide path runs towards Ilminster, with sports fields below. Turn **L**, between sports fields and town, for 200yds (183m) to yellow litter bin. Gap on **R** leads to path alongside remnant of Chard–Taunton **Canal**. Turn **R** behind tennis courts; after 250yds (229m) turn **L** into Abbots Close and on to tarred path. This leads to West Street, arriving at **Crown Inn**. Turn **R** and bear **R** into Silver Street, to reach town centre.

Ham Hill Golden Stone

4 miles (6.4km) 2hrs **Ascent:** 700ft (210m)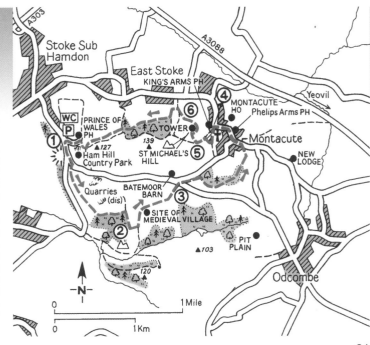
Paths: Well-trodden and sometimes muddy, 5 stiles
Suggested map: OS Explorer 129 Yeovil & Sherborne
Grid reference: ST 478167
Parking: Main car park on western escarpment of Ham Hill

Ascending the hill whose warm-coloured limestone forms the towns and villages of Somerset.

❶ Turn **R** out of car park; follow road to junction. Bear **L** then take path on **R** ('Norton Sub Hamdon'), which leads through woods around side of Ham Hill. When open field appears ahead, turn **R**, downhill. Ignore 1st gate on L and continue to 2nd.

❷ Descend grassland into small valley with hummocks of **medieval village** of Witcombe. Head up valley floor, passing to **L** of willow clump. Grassy path climbs **R-H** side of valley to field corner. Turn **L** on track leading to lane near **Batemoor Barn**.

❸ Hollow Lane descends directly opposite the barn. Stile to **R** passes along field edges, then into wood. Shortly, turn **R** to stile. Clear path runs just below top of wood, then down to edge of **Montacute village**. Turn **L** near entrance to **Montacute House**, to reach **King's Arms Inn**.

❹ Turn **L**, past church; after duck pond turn **R** on to permissive path. Kissing gate leads you to bottom of **St Michael's Hill**. Turn **L** to stile into woods.

❺ Path ahead is arduous. For gentler way up hill, turn **L** around base to descending track. Otherwise head slightly **L** up steep path, to join same track just below summit tower. The **Tower's** open and spiral staircase are worth climb. Descend spiralling track to gate at hill's foot.

❻ Turn half-**R** and go straight down field to gate leading on to track corner. Turn **L** and follow track round field corner. After 90yds (82m) take **R** fork. Earth track runs close to foot of woods, passing ruins of pump house, and diminishing to path; it then climbs steps to join higher one. Turn **R** to continue close to foot of woods until path emerges at gate. Steps lead up to **Prince of Wales pub**. Turn **L** along its lane, passing through hummocks of former quarries, to car park and start.

Cucklington Deepest Somerset

5½ miles (8.8km) 2hrs 45min **Ascent:** 600ft (180m)

Paths: Little-used field paths, which may be overgrown, 11 stiles

Suggested map: OS Explorer 129 Yeovil & Sherborne

Grid reference: ST 747298

Parking: Lay-by on former main road immediately south of A303

Up hill and down, taking in a church with over a thousand years of history.

❶ With back to A303, turn **R** on lane to where track runs ahead into wood. At far side, fenced footpath runs alongside main road. Turn **L** up path, then **R** into fenced-off path that bends **L** to **Parkhouse Farm**. After passage to **L** of buildings, turn **L** again to lane.

❷ Turn back **R**, following field edge back by farm track. Go through gate; turn **L** through gate. Heading towards Stoke Trister church, follow **L** edge of field; go straight up 2nd field, turning **R** along lane to church.

❸ Continue to stile. Go uphill past muddy track, but turn **R** alongside hedge immediately above. Follow around **Coneygore Hill**, over stile, then to 2nd; go straight down to **Stileway Farm**.

❹ Turn **L** by top of farm buildings. Continue into field track but immediately take gate above; pass along base of 2 fields, to gate by cattle trough. Head uphill, with hedge to **L**, to steeper bank around Coneygore

Hill. Turn **R** and follow banking to stile. Keep on to gap between bramble clumps; slant down **R** to gate in corner leading on to green track and then to lane near **Manor Farm**.

❺ Turn downhill past thatched cottage and red phone box; bear **R** for **Cucklington**. There are field paths on **L**, but use lane to cross valley and climb to Cucklington. Gravel track on **L** leads to Cucklington church.

❻ Pass **L** of church; cross 2 fields, passing above **Cucklington Wood**. In 3rd field slant to **R** to join track to **Clapton Farm**.

❼ After Tudor manor house track bends **R**, uphill. Turn **L** between farm buildings to gate, then turn **L** down wooded bank. Turn **R**, along base of bank, to gap in hedge. Bear **L** past power pole to field's bottom corner. Cross 2 streams; bear **L** to cross 3rd and stile beyond. Go straight up to stile by cattle trough and lane you parked on.

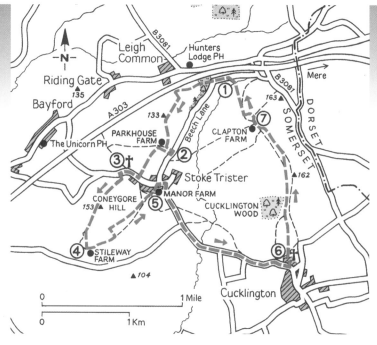

South Cadbury Cadbury Castle as Camelot?

6¾ miles (10.9km) 3hrs 30min **Ascent:** 1,000ft (300m) **2**

Paths: Well-used paths, 6 stiles
Suggested map: OS Explorer 129 Yeovil & Sherborne
Grid reference: ST 632253
Parking: Cadbury Castle car park (free), south of South Cadbury

Cadbury Castle hill fort gives wide views of Somerset and a glimpse of pre-history.

1 Turn **R** out of car park to 1st house in South Cadbury. Track leads up to **Cadbury Castle**. Ramparts and top of fort are access land; stroll around at will.

2 Return past car park. After ¼ mile (400m) pass side road on L, to stile signposted '**Sigwells**'. Walk down to reach stile and footbridge. Cross then follow **L** edge of field, then uncultivated strip. Track starts ahead, but take stile on **R** to follow field edge next to it, to gate with 2 waymarkers. Faint track leads along top of following field. At end turn down into hedged-earth track which leads out past **Whitcombe Farm** to rejoin road.

3 Turn **L** to junction below Corton Denham **Beacon**. Turn **L** to slant uphill for ¼ mile (400m). Track on R leads to open hilltop and summit **trig point**.

4 Head along steep hill rim to stile with dog slot. Continue along top of slope (Corton Denham below).

Pass modern 'tumulus' (small, covered reservoir). Above 5 large beeches slant down to waymarked gate. Green path slants down again, until gate leads to tarred lane; follow to road below.

5 Turn **L** on road, between high banks for 110yds (100m) to stile ('**Middle Ridge Lane**'). Keep to **L** of trees to field gate, with stile beyond leading into lane. Go across into stony track that climbs to ridgeline.

6 Turn **R**; walk along **Corton Ridge** with hedge on R and view on L. After 650yds (594m) Ridge Lane starts on R, but go through small gate on **L** to continue along the ridge. After small gate, green path bends around flank of **Parrock Hill**. With **Cadbury Castle** now on L, ignore 1st green track down to L. Shortly main track turns down **L** into hedge end and waymarked gate. Hedged path leads down to road.

7 Cross into road ('**South Cadbury**'). Shortly turn **R**, again for **South Cadbury**; follow road round base of **Cadbury Castle** to car park.

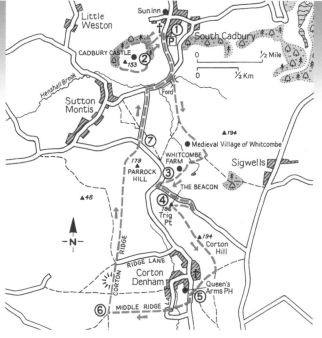

Polden Hills Edge of the Levels

4½ miles (7.2km) 2hrs 15min **Ascent:** 450ft (140m)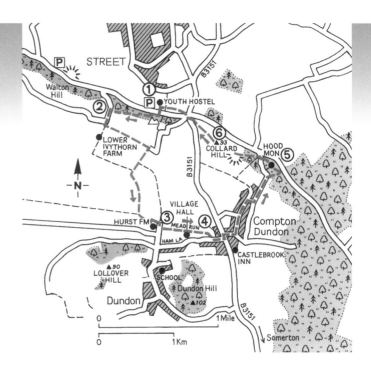

Paths: Initially steep then easy tracks and paths, 3 stiles

Suggested map: OS Explorer 141 Cheddar Gorge

Grid reference: ST 480345

Parking: Car park (free) at Street Youth Hostel, just off B3151; another car park on south side of road

From Polden's edge down on to the Somerset Levels and up again.

❶ From parking area on youth hostel side, cross and turn **R** on woodland path. Shortly smaller path descends on **L** by steps. At foot of wood turn **R**; at field corner go down short way to track which runs along base of wood to lane.

❷ Go down to **Lower Ivythorn Farm** entrance; turn **L** into track. After ½ mile (800m) this reaches corner of unsurfaced road; turn **R**. After ¼ mile (400m) track turns **L** into field. Follow edge, with ditch and fence **L**, to gate. In next field continue alongside ditch to corner. Former footpath is derelict. Take gate on **L**, then turn **R** on field track, passing **L** of Hurst Farm, to tarred lane.

❸ Turn **R** to bridleway sign on **L**. Follow green track to Ham Lane. This leads to crossroads of **B3151** in **Compton Dundon** (**Castlebrook Inn** to R).

❹ Cross busy **B3151** and pass between ancient market cross (R) and Victorian obelisk (L) into Compton Street. At 1st junction keep to **L**, towards **Hood Monument** above. As street climbs, turn **R** and **L** up lane beyond. Where it reaches woodland turn off through waymarked gate ('Reynolds Way'). Path slants up into wood. Shortly before it arrives at road, turn **L** along top of steep ground, to **Hood Monument.**

❺ Continue down through wood to minor road, with main road 50yds (46m) away on R. Ignore path descending opposite but turn **R** for few steps to footpath sign and kissing gate. Grass path heads up crest of **Collard Hill**, (wide views to L).

❻ From summit go straight on down to stile and signposted crossroads of **B3151**. Cross both roads. Ridge road signposted for youth hostel; path is just to **R**, crossing glade into woodland. Keep to **R** of hummocky ground to wood's edge; follow this path to car park.

Bruton Golden Wool

4½ miles (7.2km) 2hrs 15min **Ascent:** 500ft (150m)

Paths: Enclosed tracks, open fields, an especially muddy farmyard
Suggested map: OS Explorer 142 Shepton Mallet
Grid reference: ST 684348
Parking: Free parking off Silver Street, 50yds (46m) west of church; larger car park in Upper Backway

A walk around and above beautiful Bruton, a typical Somerset wool town.

① With church **L** and bridge **R**, head down Silver Street to car park in Coombe Street. Old packhorse bridge over River Brue leads into Lower Backway. Turn **L** for 350yds (320m), ignoring arch leading towards footbridge; take path between railed fences to 2nd footbridge. Turn **R** along river to **West End**.

② Turn **R** over river and **R** again into end of High Street; immediately turn uphill on to walled path ('Mill Dam'). At lane above turn **R** along track ('Huish Lane'). Just after footbridge fork **L**: hedged track is steep and muddy, bending **R** then **L** to lane (**Wyke Road**).

③ Turn **R**, then **R** again; after 220yds (201m) turn **R** past farm buildings on to uphill track (**Creech Hill Lane**), which becomes hedged tunnel, then emerges at **Creech Hill Farm**. Pass along front of farm and out to B3081. Turn **L** over hill crest to triangular junction.

④ Turn **R** for 40yds (37m) to public bridleway sign and gate on **R**. Go down combe below; at foot keep **L** of **Green's Combe Farm** and above intermittent wall; turn down through gate between farm buildings.

⑤ Continue down farm's access track for ¼ mile (400m) until it bends **R**. Keep ahead through field gate with blue waymarker, on to green track. After 200yds (183m), beside 3 stumps, turn downhill, to **L** of hazels, to gate. Pass through small wood to gate and waymarked track. When this emerges into open field follow fence above to join B3081. Turn **L**, uphill, to **Coombe Farm** entrance.

⑥ Ignoring stile on **L**, go through ivy-covered wall gap, then down driveway; turn **L** on to wide path under sycamores. Path rises, with bank on **L**. At open grassland, keep to **L** edge to descending path that becomes St Catherine's Lane. Weavers' cottages are on **R** as street descends into **Bruton**. Turn **L** along High Street. At end turn **R** down Patwell Street to Church Bridge.

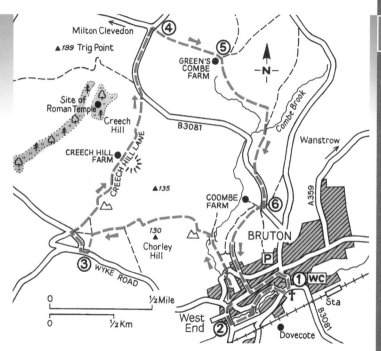

Somerset • Southwest England

Nunney Village, Castle and Combe

3 miles (4.8km) 1hr 15min **Ascent:** 100ft (30m)

Paths: Broad, riverside path, pasture, then leafy track, 8 stiles

Suggested map: OS Explorer 142 Shepton Mallet

Grid reference: ST 736456

Parking: Short-stay parking at Nunney Market Square; small lay-by at end of a public footpath 150yds (137m) up Castle Hill

Through woodland and pasture, visiting a stone-built village with a moated castle.

❶ From Nunney's Market Square cross brook and immediately turn **R** to **Nunney Castle** (entry free). Inspect castle, then return and pass **R**, across footbridge, to church. Further on, where street starts uphill, turn **L** into Donkey Lane.

❷ Follow lane past high wall on **L**, to gate with signpost. Keep ahead, leaving track after 150yds (137m) for small gate ahead into woods. Wide path leads downstream with **Nunney Brook** on **L**. After about ¾ mile (1.2km) track runs across valley.

❸ Turn **L** to cross brook; immediately turn **R** over broken stile. Continue along stream on path. After 350yds (320m) path climbs away from stream to join track above. Turn **R** on this, to cross stream on high-arched bridge. Track bends **R**, through gate: before next gate look for grey gate (**L**) with waymarking arrow.

❹ Go up **R-H** side of narrow field to field gate (no stile). Continue uphill on **L-H** edge for 50yds (46m), to stile in hedge. This, and following stiles, have waymarkers giving direction across next field. Turn half-**R** as arrow indicates, slanting up to hedge and follow it along top of field to stile at corner. At crest of broad ridge there are views ahead to hills in west.

❺ Turn **L** around field to stile in next corner. Cross, turn half-**R** and go straight across field to double stile at furthest corner. Cross and follow **L-H** edge of long field ahead. At corner cross stile between 2 gateways and turn **R**. After 400yds (366m), before end of field, watch out for stile on **R**.

❻ This leads into narrow track between over-arching hedges. It bends to **L** then **R**, then descends to become street leading into **Nunney**. Street runs down to join Donkey Lane on outward route, with church 300yds (274m) ahead.

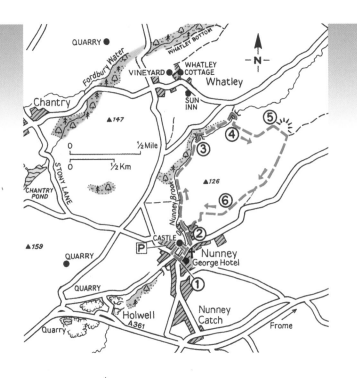

Burrow Mump On the Levels

5¼ miles (8.4km) 2hrs 15min **Ascent:** 150ft (50m)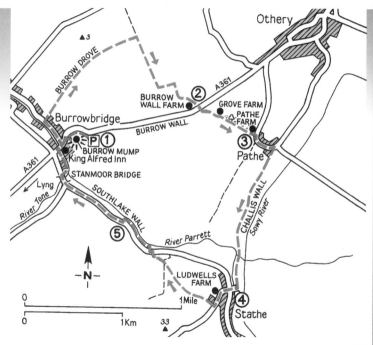

Paths: Tracks, paths, unfrequented field edges, 6 stiles
Suggested map: OS Explorer 140 Quantock Hills & Bridgwater
Grid reference: ST 360395
Parking: National Trust car park (free) at Burrow Mump

A gentle wander around the Somerset Levels near Burrowbridge leading up to a 'mump'.

❶ Gate leads on to base of **Mump**. Keep to **R** to small gate and steps down to Burrow Bridge. Before bridge turn **R** into Riverside. After 350yds (320m) turn **R** into **Burrow Drove**, which becomes tractor track. On either side and between fields are deep ditches, coated in bright green pondweed. At T-junction is 19th-century brick culvert on **L**. Turn **R** on new track, passing behind **Burrow Wall Farm**, to meet busy **A361**.

❷ 'Public footpath' sign points to track opposite. After 30yds (27m) turn **L** over stile. With bushy **Burrow Wall R**, cross field to **Grove Farm** (usually muddy). Go through 2 gates; continue along fields beside woodland on **L**. At end of 2nd field rusty gate leads up between brambles to green track: turn **R** to lane near **Pathe Farm**.

❸ Turn **R** along lane, ignoring track on R, to side-lane on **R**. Here cross bridge to hedge-gap on **R** and very narrow footbridge. Continue through several fields, with wide rhyne (ditch) on R. Near by, on **L**, is low banking of **Challis Wall**, concealing **Sowy River**. Ditch on R gradually gets smaller. When it finally ends bear **R** to **River Parrett** and follow to latticework road bridge. Cross into edge of **Stathe**.

❹ Keep ahead through village, past phone box and **Ludwells Farm**, to stile on **R** ('Macmillan Way'). Follow **R** edge of field to gate; cross to hedge opposite and follow round to **L**, to stile. Continue with hedge on R to gate, where hedged track leads to road. Turn **L**, scrambling up banking, to walk on **Southlake Wall** between road and river.

❺ As road turns away from river, rejoin it. Once across **Stanmoor Bridge** waymarker points to **R** for riverbank path to **Burrowbridge**. Turn **R** and, this time, climb to top of **Burrow Mump** for overview of entire walk and much of Somerset.

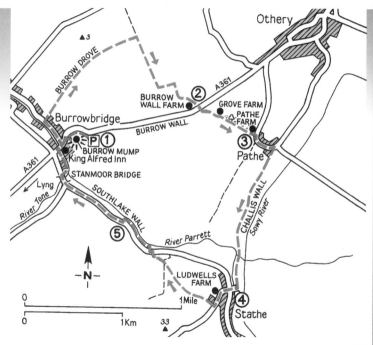

Ebbor Gorge Coleridge's Inspiration

4¾ miles (7.7km) 2hrs 30min **Ascent:** 700ft (210m)

Paths: Small paths and field edges, with a rugged descent, 9 stiles

Suggested map: OS Explorer 141 Cheddar Gorge

Grid reference: ST 521484

Parking: Lane above Wookey Hole (optional, small fee)

The small but sublime limestone gorge that inspired the poet, Samuel Taylor Coleridge.

❶ From notice-board at top end of car park descend stepped path. After clearing, turn **L** ('The Gorge'). Wide path crosses stream to another junction.

❷ Turn **R**, away from gorge; follow valley down to road. Turn **L**, passing through village of **Wookey Hole**. At end of village, road bends R; take kissing gate on **L** ('West Mendip Way' waymarker post). After 2 more kissing gates turn **L** up spur to stile and top of **Arthur's Point**.

❸ Bear **R** into woods again. Beware: hidden in brambles ahead is top of quarry crag; turn **R**, down to stile. Go down field edge to kissing gate; bear **L** between boulders back into wood. After sharp rise bear **R**, to join Lime Kiln Lane below, which bends L with path on **L** diverting through bottom of wood. This emerges at end of short field track; follow down to footpath signpost.

❹ Turn sharp **L**, on track that passes through **Model Farm**, to Tynings Lane. Turn **L** to signposted stile on your **R**. Go up with fence R, then bear **L** to gate with stile. Go straight up next, large field, aiming for gateway with tractor ruts. Track leads up through wood and field to gate. Slant upwards in same direction to another gate next to stile 100yds (91m) below field's top L corner.

❺ Small path runs along tops of 3 fields with long view across Levels to L. With stile on R and gate and horse trough in front, turn downhill with fence on R; follow fence to stile leading into **Ebbor Gorge** Nature Reserve.

❻ 2nd gate leads into wood. At junction with red arrow and sign ('Car Park') pointing forward, turn **R** into valley and go down – it narrows to rocky gully. At foot of gorge turn **R** ('Car Park'). You are now back at Point ❷ of outward walk. Cross stream, turn **L** at T-junction to wood edge and back **R** to car park.

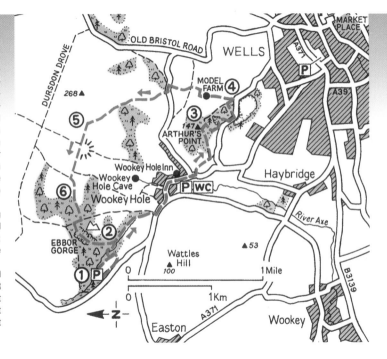

Crook Peak The Western Mendips

6 miles (9.7km) 3hrs **Ascent:** 900ft (270m)
Paths: Field edges, then wide clear paths, 6 stiles
Suggested map: OS Explorer 153 Weston-super-Mare
Grid reference: ST 392550
Parking: On road between Cross and Bleadon, west of Compton Bishop; also street parking in Cross and on A38

A high-level ridge wander in the western Mendips to Somerset's shapeliest summit.

1 Cross road to wide gate on **R** (not small gate ahead). Wide path contours round through brambly scrub, crosses ridgeline and drops through wood to its foot. Go down through gate into **Compton Bishop** and turn **L** to church.

2 Lane turns down, before church, to crossroads. Take track opposite and follow it round bend to its end. Contour round base of high slope of **Wavering Down**. Cross stile, pass through wrought-iron gate into narrow paddock, and cross another stile into large field; keep along bottom edge. At its corner keep ahead over stile, then through 2 gates, then go 40yds (37m) uphill around fence corner to another stile on same level. Follow long bottom edge of field to track and turn **R**, down to road. Turn **L** through **Cross** village.

3 At 'Give Way 150yds' sign (warning of **A38**

ahead) turn **L** up enclosed path, which turns **R** above fence, then slants up to rejoin same fence higher up. It enters woodland, running above bank of hornbeams: watch out for waymarker where path bears **R** to pass through this bank. After gate ignore stile above to stay on main track, which emerges at top of car park on **Winscombe Hill**.

4 Turn **L**, away from car park, on broad track uphill. This rises through **King's Wood**, then dips slightly to pass pantiled **Hill Farm**, before rising to trig point on **Wavering Down**. Continue with wall on **R**, walking next to wall for views over it, to cross **Barton Hill**. In dip below **Crook Peak** waymarkers point to L and R, but keep ahead to climb slightly crag-topped summit.

5 Turn **L** and (with small rocky drop to L) head down on to long gentle ridge – outcrops of limestone poke out through shallow grass of path. At railed barrier turn **R** on path back to car park.

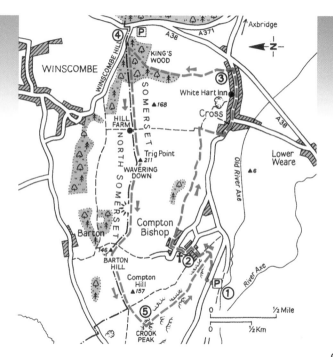

Dolebury Warren An Iron-Age Hill Fort

5¼ miles (8.4km) 2hrs 30min **Ascent:** 600ft (180m) 🔺

Paths: Wide and mostly mud-free, 4 stiles

Suggested map: OS Explorer 141 Cheddar Gorge

Grid reference: ST 444575

Parking: Pull-off near church; street parking around main Shipham crossroads

A walk through woodland and heathland on the northern rim of the Mendips.

❶ From main crossroads in centre of Shipham head uphill on Hollow Road ('**Rowberrow**'). At top bear **R** (Barn Pool), then turn **R** again (Lipiatt Lane). Continue walking up hill, then at its end keep ahead on path with waymarker for Cheddar, to descend sunken path to stream.

❷ Just before stream turn **L** on path ('**Rowberrow**'). Stay to **L** of stream (ignoring R fork) – path becomes tarred track. After 3 houses and limekiln bear **R** into forest at notice-board ('**Rowberrow Warren**').

❸ Track bends to **R**, climbing. At corner of open field turn **L** into smaller track that descends with this field above on its R. At junction keep ahead, uphill, then turn **L** on forest track with bridleway sign.

❹ After 350yds (320m) track ends; bear **L** down path with forest on R. Where it joins stony track and path below, bear **R** on stony track, with wall to L. At T-junction turn **L** to gate on **L** with National Trust sign.

❺ Follow grassy ridgeline ahead, passing along **L** side of fenced enclosure of scrubland. At its end, bear **R** ('Limestone Link' waymarker) to pass to R of tall pine clump. Emerge on to more open grassland (wide views). Highest point of ridge is rim of **Dolebury hill fort.**

❻ Green track runs down through fort and into woods below. It bends **L**, then back **R**, emerging at gate on to tarred lanes. Take lane on **R**, down to **A38**. Cross to signposted bridleway, which passes to lane. Turn **L** – ground on L consists of broken stones from disused **Churchill Quarry** below. Ignore turnings L and R and follow enclosed track down to Star.

❼ Cross **A38** on to grass track to stile; go up grassy spur above. Keep to **L** of some trees to stile; pass to **R** of football pitch, to short path out to edge of **Shipham**. Turn **R**, to village centre.

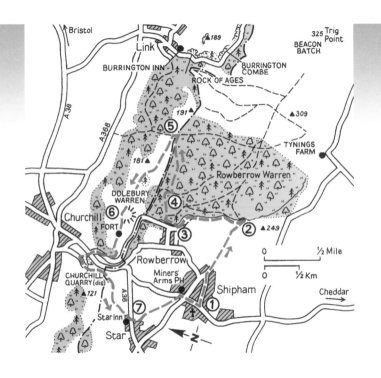

Woollard Hunstrete and Compton Dando

6¼ miles (10.1km) 3hrs 30min **Ascent:** 700ft (210m)

Paths: Tracks, field paths, woodland paths, and byways, 15 stiles

Suggested map: OS Explorer 155 Bristol & Bath

Grid reference: ST 632644

Parking: Street parking near bridge in Woollard; also opposite pub in Compton Dando (Point **6**)

Serenity in a rich landscape nestling between the cities of Bristol and Bath.

1 At southern end of **Woollard** bear **R** at 'Circular Walk' sign. Byway initially underwater; path parallels it on **R**. After byway becomes Birchwood Lane, turn **L** into **Lord's Wood**, on path (Three Peaks Way). Go downhill, crossing track, to pool. Pass to **L** of this, to waymarker and track junction. Track opposite leads up to edge of wood.

2 Turn **R**; drop to hidden footbridge under trees. Head uphill, passing R-H edge of plantation, to **Pete's Gate** beside corner of **Hunstrete Plantation**. Turn **L** to field gate. Right of way bears **R**, but, with no sign of path, keep ahead to lane and turn **R** into Hunstrete.

3 Turn **L** beside Cottage No 5. Ignoring waymarking arrow, go down R-H side of field to stile into **Common Wood**. Track ahead passes through paintball sports area. Where it crosses stream and bends **L**, take waymarked path rising to top of wood. Pass through

small col with lone ash tree, down to hedge corner. Go straight downhill to signpost; turn **R** to join lane at **Marksbury Vale**.

4 Turn **L** towards **Court Farm**; before buildings, turn **R** over stile, and take R-H track for 100yds (91m) to stile. Pass to R-H side of farm buildings to enclosed track following **Bathford Brook**. Head downstream to track at **Tuckingmill**.

5 Follow track past manor house to ford. Cross footbridge and turn **R**, alongside stream, which is again lost of underwater byway – rejoin as it emerges; it leads to road, with **Compton Dando** away to **L**.

6 Turn **R** into Church Lane; go through lychgate. Stile leads down. Turn **L** behind mill house and pass to **L** of mill pond, to footbridge over **River Chew**.

7 Bear **L** into woodland ('Park Copse'). At top follow R-H edge of field round to stile. In lane beyond turn **L**; it becomes hedged track and runs alongside tiny gorge as it descends to **Woollard**.

Hengistbury Head Heights and Huts

3¼ miles (5.3km) 2hrs **Ascent:** 109ft (33m)

Paths: Grass, tarmac road, soft sand, woodland track, some steps
Suggested map: OS Explorer OL 22 New Forest
Grid reference: SZ 163912
Parking: Car park (fee) at end of road, signed 'Hengistbury Head' from B3059

An easy coastal loop with much to see.

❶ From corner of car park take grassy path towards sea, with fenced-off lines of **Double Dikes** to L. At sea-edge you can see to towers of **Bournemouth**, chalky Foreland and Durlston Head to west; Christchurch Bay and Isle of Wight are to east.

❷ Turn **L** and follow road along cliffs. Priory Church in Christchurch dominates view inland across harbour, with St Catherine's Hill behind. Follow road up hill. Pause to admire boggy pond to R, home to rare natterjack toad. Road narrows; climb up some steps, passing numbered post marking **Stour Valley Way**. As you climb, views back along coast are fabulous; also views across shallows of **Christchurch Harbour**, with windsurfers and sailing dinghies.

❸ On top of **Warren Hill** viewing platform indicates you're 75 miles (120km) from Cherbourg and 105 miles (168km) from Jersey. Keep **R** along path, passing deserted coastguard station and following top

of cliffs. Descend into deep hollow, where sea appears to break through. Keep straight on, following curve of head, with views across to Needles. At end, path turns down through trees; descend steps. Walk along sand on sea side of beach huts to point. Stone groynes form little bays.

❹ At end of spit you're not far from opposite shore (ferry runs across to pub from end of pier, passed further on). Turn round end of point, passing old Black House; walk up inner side of spit, overlooking harbour.

❺ If you've had enough beach and breeze, catch land train back to car park from here (times vary seasonally). Otherwise, join metalled road which curves round to **R** past freshwater marsh and lagoon.

❻ At post marked '19' turn **R** on to sandy path and follow through woods, crossing small ditch, to emerge back on road. Turn **R**, passing reedbeds on R and bird sanctuary on L. Continue past thatched barn and follow road to **café**, **ranger station** and car park.

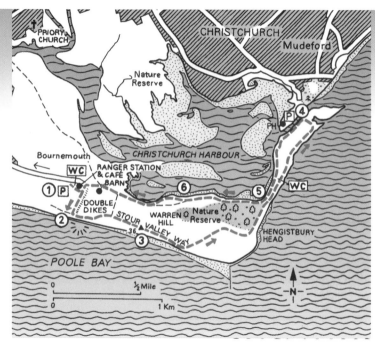

Horton The Rebel King

7½ miles (12.1km) 4hrs **Ascent:** 426ft (130m) ▲**2**
Paths: Field paths, tracks, some road, 15 stiles
Suggested map: OS Explorer OL 22 New Forest; Explorer 118 Shaftesbury & Cranborne Chase
Grid reference: SU 034072 (on Explorer 118)
Parking: Lay-by with phone box, just west of Horton

A luscious landscape, where once a rebel was roused.

❶ Go towards village; turn **L** over stile by pump. Head towards **Horton Tower**, crossing 2 more stiles. Go up hill, diagonally **L**. Cross fence at top corner; turn **R** to view tower.

❷ Retrace steps; stay on track through gate into **Ferndown Forest**. After ¼ mile (400m) join firmer track. Shortly, turn **R** between trees. Cross stream and track to gate.

❸ Pass this, go through bank and turn **L** along forest ride. Turn **R** before edge of wood; follow path for ¾ mile (1.2km). Bear **L** at bottom, down track. Turn **L** at road; pass **Paradise Farmhouse**.

❹ Turn **L** between houses; follow road to **Holt Lodge Farm**. With buildings L, bear half-**R** across yard to lane.

❺ At end bear **L** into field, (hedge to R). Cross stile; go through gate to **Early's Farm**. Turn immediately **L** to gate, and **R**, in front of house, into lane. At junction

after **Chapel Farm**, turn **L**, signed 'Long House'. Turn **R** at gate; cross stile. Bear **L** around field, cross stile by bungalow and another to road.

❻ Turn **L**, then **R** into lane by **Pee Wee Lodge**. Keep straight on at junction; fork **R** into **Grixey Farm**. Follow waymarker up hill, crossing 2 stiles. With copse L, go up field. Cross stile and turn **L** on to road.

❼ After ½ mile (800m) bear **L** ('Monmouth's Ash Farm'); take path to **R** of bungalow. Keep straight on bridleway over heath and down into woodland. After 1 mile (1.6km) track emerges from woods.

❽ Past **Woodlands Manor Farm** turn **L** along road with fence. Bear **R** beside lake; stay on road. After it becomes track, look for 2 stiles in hedge on R, just after farm. Cross and go diagonally across field to another stile. Cross top of next field and stile, turning **R** to road.

❾ Turn **L** through **Haythorne**; before road descends, go **R**, through trees, to gate and down field, to vineyard. Turn **L** and **L** again to return to car.

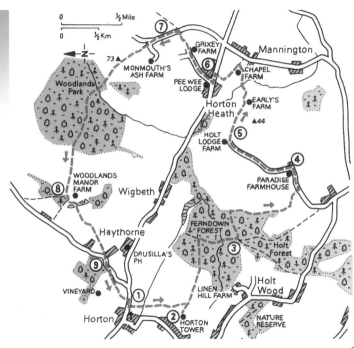

Studland Sand and Heath

7 miles (11.3km) 4hrs **Ascent:** 132ft (40m)

Paths: Sandy beach, muddy heathland tracks, verges, no stiles
Suggested map: OS Explorer OL 15 Purbeck & South Dorset
Grid reference: SZ 033835
Parking: Knoll car park, by visitor centre, just off B3351

Easy walking through a nature reserve over beach and heath.

❶ From car park go past visitor centre to sea. Turn **L** and walk up beach for about 2 miles (3.2km). Dunes hide edge of heath to **L**, but there are views to Tennyson Down on Isle of Wight, and cliffs of Bournemouth curve away ahead. Continue round tip of sand bar into **Shell Bay**. Poole opens out ahead – more precisely, spit of Sandbanks with good views of nature reserve island of Brownsea, with Branksea Castle at eastern end.

❷ Turn inland at **South Haven Point**, joining road by phone box. Pass boatyard and toll booth; bear **R** at gate on to bridleway, leading down to houseboats. Turn **L** along tranquil inner shore of Poole Harbour and past **Bramble Bush Bay**. Choose any of various tracks leading back up to road. Cross over and follow verge until end of woods on **L**; pick up broad muddy track on heath. After ½ mile (800m) this bends **L**, with

views across to Little Sea. Where track bends sharply **R** to meet road, stay straight ahead on footpath for few more paces.

❸ Cross road by bus stop and head down track, indicated by fingerpost. Go past marshy end of **Studland Heath** and up to junction by **Greenland Farm**. Bear **L** and, just round next corner, turn **L** through gate on to heath. Go straight along old hedge-line, pass barn on **L**, and reach fingerpost.

❹ Turn **L** across heath (not shown on fingerpost), aiming for distant lump of **Agglestone**. Go through gate by another fingerpost; continue along muddy track over top, passing **Agglestone** away to **R**. Go down into woods, turn **R** over footbridge and pass through gate into lane. Pass several houses then, where blue markers indicate public bridleway, turn **L** into field. Head diagonally **R** into green lane and go through gate at bottom. Turn **L** along verge, pass **Knoll House Hotel** and turn **R** at signpost to return to car park.

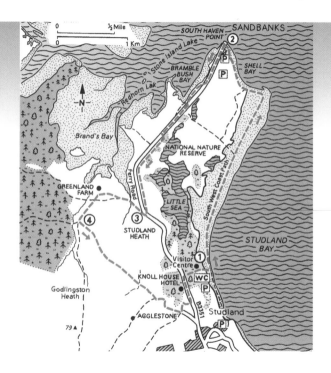

Swanage The Extraordinary Collector

4¼ miles (6.8km) 3hrs **Ascent:** 509ft (155m) ▲
Paths: Grassy paths, rocky tracks, pavements, 4 stiles
Suggested map: OS Explorer OL 15 Purbeck & South Dorset
Grid reference: SZ 031773
Parking: Durlston Country Park (charge)

A coastal town that not only exported stone but imported it too.

❶ Take footpath below visitor centre car park, signed ('**lighthouse**'). Steps lead down through trees. With sea ahead, follow path to **R**, joining coastal path. Keep **R**, towards **lighthouse**, down path. Climb up other side, looking back and down towards **Tilly Whim Caves**. Pass **lighthouse**, turn **R**, then go through kissing gate; follow path with butterfly markers up steep side of **Round Down**.

❷ At top bear **R**, heading inland and parallel with wall. Go down slope, through gate and across footbridge; turn up **R**. At wooden gate turn **L** over stile, following butterfly marker. After another stile you can see Purbeck Hills ahead. Cross stile and go down track. Beyond stile by farm, track narrows and starts climbing. Continue ahead on to road and follow into town (prominent church before you).

❸ Turn **R** on to main road. Continue along street;

look out for metal plaque above front door of No 22A, home of Taffy Evans, who died with Captain Scott on return from South Pole; elaborate Wesley memorial; and **Town Hall** with Wren frontage, donated by George Burt who collected stonework from old buildings.

❹ At square bear **L** beside Heritage Centre, towards harbour. Turn **R** and pass entrance to **pier**. Keep **L** at yellow marker; bear **R**, up hill, past modern apartment block and stone tower, to **Peveril Point**, with coastguard station.

❺ Turn **R**; walk up grassy slope along top of cliffs. Take path in top corner and follow Victoria's head markers to road. Turn **L** through area of Victorian villas. Erosion of coastal path means well-signed detour here, along street, down to **L** and **L** into woodland ('**lighthouse**'). Follow path for about ½ mile (800m) along cliff top to **Durlston Head**. Pass **Durlston Castle** on **L** and turn down to examine stone globe of world. Climb back up hill to return to car park.

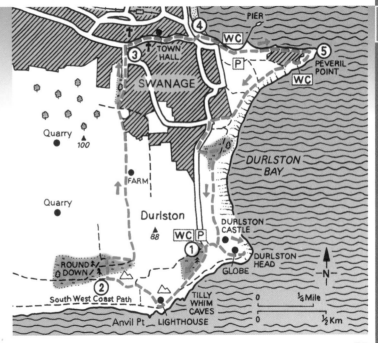

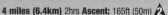

65 Cranborne Chase The Royal Forest

4 miles (6.4km) 2hrs **Ascent:** 165ft (50m)
Paths: Woodland paths and tracks, quiet roads, farm paths, 3 stiles
Suggested map: OS Explorer 118 Shaftesbury & Cranborne Chase
Grid reference: SU 003194
Parking: Garston Wood car park (free), on Bowerchalke road 2 miles (3.2km) north of Sixpenny Handley

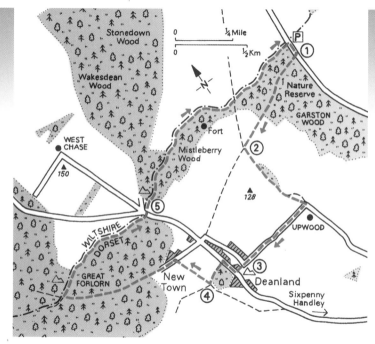

Extensive plantations on the rolling landscape of a Norman royal hunting forest provide superb walking.

1 Go through gate in corner and take track leading up through woods. Go ahead through kissing gate emerging at corner of field. Keep **R**, up edge of field; continue straight on.

2 At junction of tracks turn **L**; walk alongside hedge, on waymarked bridleway, through rolling farmland. Muddy farm track leads downhill. Where it sweeps **L** into farm, go ahead on grassy track. Pass cow byres (L), with **Upwood** farmhouse in trees ahead; turn **R** along lane. Continue through gate, along avenue of sycamores between high banks and hedges.

3 Pass house on R; bear **L** on steep path straight down hill to road, in **Deanland**. Turn **R**, pass phone box and reach gate on **L** (yellow marker). Go through, bear diagonally **R** across small field to cross stile, then

bear **L** up edge of field (woods L).

4 Look for stile on L, but turn directly **R** here; cross field, parallel with road. Over brow of hill ahead, settlement of **New Town** can be seen. Head for stile in bottom corner of field. Turn **L** up lane, which becomes woodland track. Follow for ½ mile (800m). By entrance to conifer wood (**Great Forlorn**), look for yellow marker and turn **R** up hill. After steep climb it levels, with fields on L. Keep straight on with good views to **West Chase** house, at head of its own valley. Descend steadily; cross stile to road by lodge house.

5 Cross straight over on to broad track and immediately turn up to **R** on narrow path beside fence. Follow straight up hill through woods – it levels out towards top, with fields on L. At junction of tracks keep **L** then bear **R**, continuing along edge of wood, and eventually descending to reach road. Turn **R** to return to car park at **Garston Wood**.

done it

Badbury Rings Roads and Residents

7½ miles (12.1km) 4hrs **Ascent:** 459ft (140m) ⚠
Paths: Farm tracks, roads, grassy lanes and fields, 15 stiles
Suggested map: OS Explorer 118 Shaftesbury & Cranborne Chase
Grid reference: ST 959031
Parking: Car park (donation) at Badbury Rings, signposted off B3082 from Wimborne to Blandford

An easy, longish walk on the edge of the Kingston Lacey Estate.

❶ Walk up hill to **Badbury Rings**, then head down track by which you drove in. Cross **B3082** and go down road towards **Shapwick** – its straightness gives away its Roman origins. Pass **Crab Farm**, with Charborough Tower on distant horizon.

❷ At junction with Park Lane turn **R**, then **R** again by Elm Tree Cottage to go up Swan Lane (grassy track). Turn **L** over stile before gate. Go over field, cross stile, and along edge of next field. Cross stile into yard of **Bishops Court Dairy**; turn **R** past 1st barn. At gates bear **L** over stile, then **R** across stile, heading for stile half-way along hedge. Cross and bear **R** to top corner of field.

❸ Cross stile and turn **L** down broad bridleway. After about ½ mile (800m) pass line of trees. Turn **R**, up track between high hedges (following blue public bridleway marker). Continue downhill. Follow track to

L, by side of stream.

❹ Go through gate and reach church on your **L**. Continue towards **Tarrant Abbey Farm** barns. Go **L** through gate and continue diagonally across field to track between fences. Follow uphill, passing above farmhouse. At top of track cross stile and go over next field. Cross road and walk down edge of field. Cross another road into green lane. Bear **L** across stile, then diagonally across field. Go through gate on to road and turn **R**.

❺ Walk on to old **Crawford Bridge**, just to admire it. Retrace steps and turn **R** at footpath sign. Cross stile and walk straight across meadows for 1 mile (1.6km). Reach fence on **L**; walk around it to gate. Go through and follow track to **R**. Cross stile behind farm and walk along road into village.

❻ Pass **Anchor pub** and turn **L**, passing Piccadilly Lane (R-H side). Go straight up road, now retracing route back to car park at **Badbury Rings**.

Ashmore Roaming the Woods

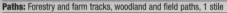

5¾ miles (9.2km) 3hrs Ascent: 427ft (130m)

Paths: Forestry and farm tracks, woodland and field paths, 1 stile

Suggested map: OS Explorer 118 Shaftesbury & Cranborne Chase

Grid reference: ST 897167

Parking: At Washers Pit entrance to Ashmore Wood

A gentle amble through plantations of mixed woodland to a village highpoint.

❶ With back to road, walk past gate; follow forestry road as it curves past **Washers Pit Coppice** on L and **Balfour's Wood** on R. After ½ mile (800m) ignore crossing bridleway and stay ahead on track. You're now in **Stubhampton Bottom**, following winding valley through trees.

❷ Where main track swings up to L, keep ahead, following blue public bridleway marker, on rutted track along valley floor. Path from **Stony Bottom** feeds in from L – keep straight on. Where area of exposed hillside appears on L, follow blue markers on to narrower track to **R**, which runs down through woodland parallel and below forestry road. At **Hanging Coppice**, fingerpost shows where **Wessex Ridgeway** path feeds in from R – again, keep ahead. Path soon rises to emerge at corner of field.

❸ Turn **L** at fence (following blue marker); walk uphill.

Follow path along edge of forest, with good views to south east of rolling hills and secretive valleys.

❹ After ¾ mile (1.2km) turn **L** at marked junction of tracks and walk through woods. Cross track and keep straight on, following marker, to meet track. Go straight on, following signs for **Wessex Ridgeway**, and passing under beech tree. Go through old gate. Continue up track for about 1 mile (1.6km), through farmland and across exposed open hilltop, with houses of **Ashmore** appearing. At end of track turn **R**; walk into village to duck pond.

❺ Retrace route but stay on road out of village, passing **Manor Farm** (R) and heading downhill. Just before road narrows, bear **L** through gate (blue marker). Walk along top of field, pass gate on L and bear down to **R** to lower of 2 gates at far side. Cross stile and walk ahead on broad green track. Go through gate into woods; immediately turn **R**, following steep bridleway down side of hill to car park.

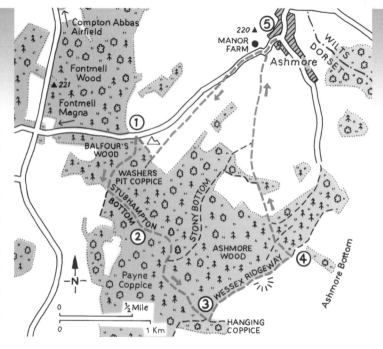

Compton Abbas Wildflowers and Butterflies

4½ miles (7.2km) 2hrs **Ascent:** 820ft (250m)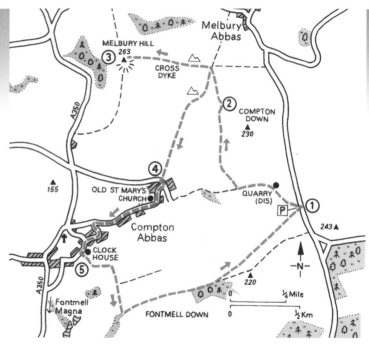
Paths: Downland tracks, muddy bridleway, village lanes, 3 stiles
Suggested map: OS Explorer 118 Shaftesbury & Cranborne Chase
Grid reference: ST 886187
Parking: Car park on road south of Shaftesbury, near Compton Abbas Airfield

Over the preserved downs around Compton Abbas, in search of butterflies and wild flowers.

❶ Take rough track from bottom **R** corner of car park, walking downhill towards **Compton Abbas**. Pass old chalk **quarry** and continue downhill. Turn **R** up steps; cross stile to **Compton Down**. Bear **L** and uphill towards fence. Follow track that contours round, just below top of hill, heading towards saddle between down and **Melbury Hill**.

❷ Pass steep, natural amphitheatre to L, go across saddle and turn **L** at fence. Follow to top of **Melbury Hill**. Pass scar of ancient **cross dyke**, on L as you climb; look down other side to Melbury Abbas church.

❸ **Trig point** marks top of hill, with fantastic views all around, including Shaftesbury to north and ridges of Hambledon Hill to south east. Retrace route downhill, with views over Melbury Down and to Compton Abbas Airfield. Turn **R** on to farm track. After

short distance bear **L**, down steep path, to gate. Go through and bear immediately **L** through 2nd gate. Go straight along muddy field edge towards **Compton Abbas**. Pass through gate on to road.

❹ Turn **L** and follow road **R** round sharp bend. Pass tower of original church, in small graveyard. Continue along lane, passing houses, with spire of modern church ahead in trees. Descend between hedges; turn **L** at junction. Follow winding road through bottom of village, passing thatched cottages.

❺ Pass **Clock House**; turn **L** up bridleway ('Gore Clump'). Gravel track gives way to tree-lined lane between fields. Go through gate and continue straight on. Cross stile by gate and continue ahead along edge of field. In corner, turn **L** along fence and walk up track above trees to gate. Pass through this on to **Fontmell Down**. Continue ahead on rising track. After ½ mile (800m) ignore stile to R and keep ahead along fence to top of hill and stile into car park.

79

Dorset • Southwest England

Hambledon Hill A Famous Landmark

4½ miles (7.2km) 3hrs **Ascent:** 541ft (165m)

Paths: Village, green and muddy lanes, bridleways, hillside, 6 stiles
Suggested map: OS Explorer 118 Shaftesbury & Cranborne Chase
Grid reference: ST 860124
Parking: Lay-by opposite Church of St Mary's

Take the gentle route up a famous sculpted landmark.

❶ With church to **L**, walk up street. Pass farmhouse on corner of Main Street and Frog Lane. Cross road into lane opposite (Courteney Close). Pass converted chapel, fork **L** and go through gate. Keep **R** along hedge. Where gardens end keep straight ahead through gate and across field.

❷ Turn **R** at fence, cross stile and turn **L**. Go through gate and bear **L** up grassy lane between hedges. Pass **Park Farm** and keep ahead. At junction bear **R** into **Bessells Lane**.

❸ At end of **Bessells Lane**, by **Lynes Cottage**, bear **R** and immediately **L** up muddy bridleway, keeping with line of trees to **L**. At top go through gate; bear **L** down narrow lane. At road turn **L** and head into **Child Okeford**. Just past post box turn **L** and cross stile. Bear **R** along edge of park, towards church tower. At fence turn **L**.

❹ Cross drive and keep straight on (glimpses of chimneys of Victorian manor house to **L**). At corner cross stile and keep ahead down path. Cross stone stile by road and immediately turn **L** up lane, which becomes track, climbing steeply through trees.

❺ Pass millennium **totem pole** and follow lane **R** and uphill. Go through gate and keep straight on up. Path levels out below earthworks that ring top of hill. Go through gate, emerge from track and go straight on up hill, through gate and across bridleway.

❻ At trig point turn **L** to explore ancient settlement. Return to trig point, turn **L** over top of hill and go down slope, following bridleway.

❼ Meet track by wall at bottom. Turn **L** and go through gate, with village ahead. Follow track down to cricket pavilion. Go through gate and turn **R**, on to road. Follow down past thatched barn and turn **R** to return to car. Alternatively, turn **L** at pavilion, and soon turn **R** by Hill View Cottage, to **pub**.

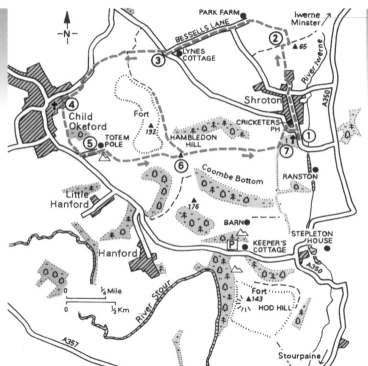

done it

Fiddleford Ancient Mills and a Manor House

5¼ miles (8.4km) 3hrs Ascent: 429ft (150m)

Paths: Grassy paths, muddy woodland tracks, a rutted lane, roadside walking, pavements, 9 stiles

Suggested map: OS Explorer 129 Yeovil & Sherborne

Grid reference: ST 781135

Parking: Signposted Sturminster Newton Mill, off A357 just west of Old Town Bridge to south of town

Two ancient mills and an extraordinary manor house, along the banks of the River Stour.

❶ Go past mill and over bridges, to **R** of pond, and through gate into field. Keep **L** up edge, parallel with **Stour**. Go through gate and up avenue of trees. Turn **R** along path, then go past playground into Ricketts Lane. Cross high street; turn **R**.

❷ Turn **L** by Old Malt House, to **church**. At end of churchyard bear **R**, through gate, down steps and into lane, bending **L**. Take path (**R**) to **Fiddleford Mill**. Go through gate and over field, above river. Cross stile; bear **L** along hedge. Continue ahead. At far **R-H** corner cross 2 footbridges and mill-race; bear **R**, past mill. Go down drive, turn **R** and **R** again through car park to **Fiddleford Manor**. Return to lane; turn **R**.

❸ At main road turn **R**; cross to bridleway, walking uphill into **Piddles Wood**. At top turn **R** on to track; follow round hill. Descend, passing 2 fingerposts. Go through gate into car park; bear **L** to road.

❹ Turn **R** and immediately **L** through farmyard ('Broad Oak'). Go ahead through 2 fields into lane. At end turn **L** down road.

❺ At bottom turn **R** down muddy, overgrown lane – **Gipsy's Drove**. Follow for ¾ mile (1.2km). Turn **R** through gate before farm. At bottom go through gate and straight over field. Cross stile, then go straight on down field edge. Cross stile on to path. Bear **R** along tree line; cross 2 stiles to lane.

❻ Turn **L**; in **Newton**, turn **L** then **R** into Hillcrest Close. Where this bends **R**, go straight down lane. Climb fence (by yellow marker); continue down field, with hedge to **R**. Leave via gate at bottom, cross **A357** and turn **R**. After town sign turn **L** up track ('Newton Farm'). At fingerpost cross stile on **R**; walk across field. Cross stile, go through woods behind barn, and down steps by fence to another stile. Bear **R** on road then **L** through gate. Cross picnic area to car park.

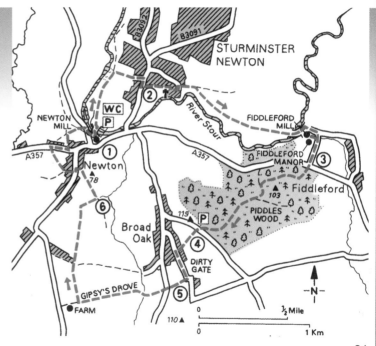

71 Ibberton Living on the Edge

Dorset • Southwest England

4¼ miles (6.8km) 2hrs **Ascent:** 591ft (180m) ▲

Paths: Quiet roads, muddy bridleways, field paths, 2 stiles

Suggested map: OS Explorer 117 Cerne Abbas & Bere Regis

Grid reference: ST 791071

Parking: Car park at Ibberton Hill picnic site

From the tops of Bulbarrow Hill to the valley floor and back, via an atmospheric church.

❶ Turn **L** along road, following route of **Wessex Ridgeway**, with Ibberton below R. Road climbs gradually, with **masts on Bulbarrow Hill** ahead.

❷ After 1 mile (1.6km) pass car park on L. At junction bear **R** and immediately **R** again ('Stoke Wake'). Pass another car park on R (woods of **Woolland Hill** on R). Pass **radio masts** to L and reach small gate into field on **R**, near end of wood. Before taking it, go extra few steps to road junction ahead for view of escarpment to west.

❸ Go through gate and follow uneven bridleway down. Glimpse spring-fed lake through trees on R. At bottom path swings **L** to gate. Go through, on to road. Turn **R**, continuing downhill. Follow road into **Woolland**, passing **Manor House** (L) and Old Schoolhouse (R).

❹ Just beyond entrance to **Woolland House** turn **R** into lane and immediately **L** through kissing gate. Path immediately forks. Take **L-H** track, down through marshy patches and young sycamores. Posts with yellow footpath waymarkers lead straight on across meadow, with **Chitcombe Down** up to R. Cross footbridge over stream. Go straight on to cross road. Keeping straight on, go through kissing gate in hedge. Bear **L** down field, cross stile and continue down. Cross footbridge and stile to bear **L** across next field. Go through gate to road junction. Walk straight up road ahead and follow it **R**, into Ibberton. Bear **R** to **Crown Inn**.

❺ Continue up road through village. Path becomes steep. Steps lead up to **church**. Continue up steep path. Cross road and go straight ahead through gate. Keep straight on along fence, climbing steadily. Cross under power lines; bear **L** up next field. Turn **L** up field edge, then go through gate at top on to road, finally turning **L** to return to car park.

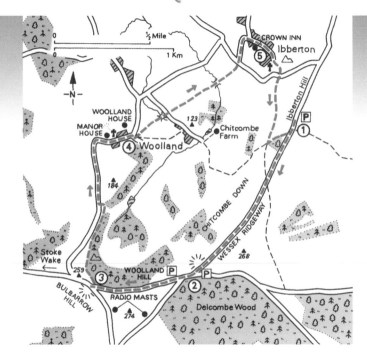

Higher Melcombe A Lost Village

5 miles (8km) 2hrs 30min **Ascent:** 443ft (135m)
Paths: Farmland, woodland track, ancient bridleway, road, 13 stiles
Suggested map: OS Explorer 117 Cerne Abbas & Bere Regis
Grid reference: ST 765031
Parking: Small parking area on north side of village hall

A hilly rural circuit, where, centuries ago, labour economics determined settlement.

❶ Turn up road and go immediately **L** down waymarked path. Cross stile, bear **R** down edge of field and cross stile at bottom. Continue straight up next field, cross stile and road to go through gate. Keep straight on to pair of stiles in hedge.

❷ Go through stiles then bear **R**, across field. Descend and go **R**, through gate in corner. Follow track beside hedge; go through gate and bend **L**.

❸ Go into **farm**; turn immediately **L** through furthest of 3 gates ('**Wessex Ridgeway**'). Walk along edge of field, above wood. Go through gate and keep ahead along top of ridge (superb views over Blackmoor Vale). Track descends abruptly. Turn **R**, through gate, to crossroads of tracks at **Dorsetshire Gap**.

❹ Turn **L** down bridleway through deep cleft ('**Higher Melcombe**'). Keep straight on through 3 fields. Ridges and hummocks in field to R are only sign of medieval village. Pass **Higher Melcombe farm**, then go through gate and turn **L**, on to minor road. Bear **R**; walk down avenue of trees (hill track leads to **Giant's Grave** on R). Descend past houses to junction.

❺ Turn **L**; walk on road into **Melcombe Bingham**. Pass houses then turn **R**. Go through gate to take path straight ahead across field. Pass end of strip of woodland and maintain direction up fence towards hut. Cross fence at top. Continue ahead, down field towards **Bingham's Melcombe**. Cross stile and turn **R**. Follow drive round and down to church.

❻ Retrace route to stile; keep straight on past, up field. Before end turn **L** through gate; bear **R** along path. Where this divides keep **L**. Go through gate and descend on track. Go straight ahead to cross footbridge. Keep straight on, bear **R** over stile in fence and continue down field. At bulging trees turn **L** over stile. Keep ahead then cross stile on to road. Turn **R** to return to car.

Higher Bockhampton By Hardy's Cottage

5 miles (8km) 2hrs **Ascent:** 328ft (100m)

Paths: Woodland and heathland tracks, muddy field paths and bridleways, firm paths, road, 15 stiles

Suggested map: OS Explorer 117 Cerne Abbas & Bere Regis

Grid reference: SY 725921

Parking: Thorncombe Wood (donations) below Hardy's Cottage

Across wooded heath and farmland to where Thomas Hardy, quite literally, left his heart.

❶ Take steep woodland path to **R** of display boards ('**Hardy's Cottage**'). Turn **L** at fingerpost; follow route to crossroads of tracks, marked by monument. Turn **L** for **Hardy's Cottage**.

❷ Retrace route up behind cottage; bear **L** ('Rushy Pond'). At crossroads take path ('Norris Mill'). Where path forks bear **R**. Cross track then head down between rhododendrons. Emerge on to heathland; stay on path. Follow markers to **R**. Descend, cross stile and bear **R**. Cross pair of stiles; turn **L** up field, towards house.

❸ Cross road on to farm track. Bear **R** before barns, cross stile and continue up track. After gate bear **R** over field. Cross pair of stiles in hedge, then fields and drive, passing **Duddle Farm** (L). Cross bridge and stile down into field. Go straight on; bear **L**, following track round hill. Cross stile by converted barn; walk up drive. At fingerpost keep straight on through gate

('**Lower Bockhampton**'). Bear **L** through another gate then walk down field to gate at far corner. Go through and straight on (river L). Go through farmyard to road.

❹ Turn **L** by **Bridge Cottage**. Cross stream; immediately turn **R**, on to causeway. After ½ mile (800m) turn **R** ('**Stinsford**'). Walk up and turn **L** into churchyard, just below church. Pass **church** (L), and **Hardy graves** (R). Hardy's heart was buried here. Leave by top gate and walk up road. Pass piggery and turn **R** along road. Turn **L** at end to main road by house.

❺ Turn **R**, up road. After entrance to **Birkin House**, bear **L** through gate and **R** on to path through woodland, parallel with road. Descend, cross stile and bear **L** to fingerpost. Go through gate and bear diagonally **R** up field ('**Higher Bockhampton**'). At top corner keep on through gate and turn **R** towards barn. Pass this and bear **R** on to track to road. Turn **L**, **R** by post box, and **R** again to car park.

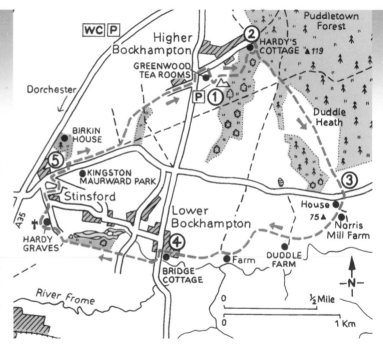

Osmington The White Horse

4 miles (6.4km) 2hrs **Ascent:** 568ft (173m)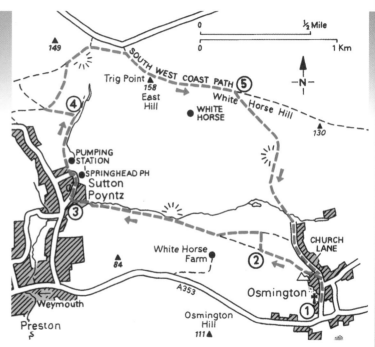

Paths: Farm and village lanes, woodland paths, field paths, 9 stiles
Suggested map: OS Explorer OL 15 Purbeck & South Dorset
Grid reference: SY 724829
Parking: Church Lane in Osmington, just off A353

Osmington's white horse is the only one depicting a rider – King George III.

❶ From **Osmington church** walk down street of pretty thatched cottages. At junction keep on down **Church Lane**. Opposite Forge Barn, at end of wall, turn **L** up steep flight of steps ('**Sutton Poyntz**'). Path rises through woodland. After 2nd set of steps bear **R** on path which undulates through trees. Cross stile and continue straight on to end of field.

❷ Cross stile and turn immediately **R** to cross 2nd stile and walk down field. Turn **L** through gate; head across field. Cross farm track and bear ahead and **R**. Cross pair of stiles and continue along bottom of (**White Horse** to **R**). Continue though gap. At end of next field bear **L**, through gateway, then straight on (yellow marker), towards **Sutton Poyntz**. Veer **R**, cross stream and bear **L** through gate. Follow path to stile and continue to road.

❸ Turn **R**, pass Mill House and mill on L. Pass village pond and **Springhead pub** on R. Bear **L** and **R** up lane by Springfield Cottage. Go through gate and follow track ahead. Go through another gate, with **pumping station** on R, below bottom of steep combe where spring emerges.

❹ Cross stile by gate; turn **L** up grassy lane. About half-way up hill turn **R**, up track (upper of 2) that leads to top above combe (great views along valley and down to Weymouth Bay and Portland). Keep **R** on green track, go through gate and keep **L** along field edge. Follow path to **R** and walk up field (lane soon joins from L). Stay on this track past trig point. Go through gate and keep straight on (good view to strip lynchets on hillside ahead).

❺ Go through gate and bear down to **R** ('**Osmington**'). Track leads down hill, through gate – look back to see **White Horse** again. Follow lane back up through village to car.

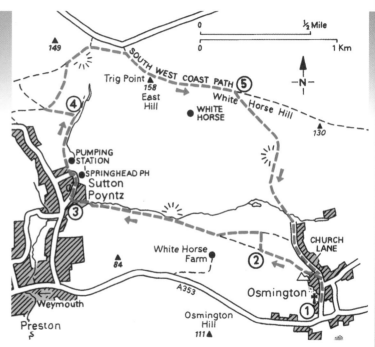

Purse Caundle In the Doghouse

5 miles (8km) 2hrs **Ascent:** 427ft (130m)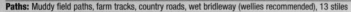

Paths: Muddy field paths, farm tracks, country roads, wet bridleway (wellies recommended), 13 stiles

Suggested map: OS Explorer 129 Yeovil & Sherborne

Grid reference: ST 695175

Parking: Limited space by war memorial, Purse Caundle

Over hill and down valley from a village dominated by a fine manor house.

❶ Park your car by **church**. Walk up street to admire **manor house**. Return, pass phone box and turn **L** through gate. Go up edge of field, cross stile and turn **R** to continue on this line, up through gateway and across another field. After 2nd gateway bear **R** up field. Cross stile in corner and turn **R**. Cross stile and pass lake to **L**. Cross stile at far side; bear **R** along field edge.

❷ Cross stile at corner and go on down edge of field. Path curves down and up to gate. Go through gate and swing **L**, up bridleway. This narrows and is shared with stream. Go through gate and keep straight on up hill. Go through gate in top corner; follow muddy track. Becomes hedged lane; follow for ½ mile (800m) to pass **Manor Farm**. Continue through gate.

❸ Turn **L** at fingerpost over stile. Bear **L** down field to cross 3 stiles and footbridge in middle of hedge.

Head diagonally **L** down next field. Cross pair of stiles and footbridge in corner; immediately turn **R** over stile and footbridge. Walk ahead up field edge.

❹ At top turn **R**, then bear **R** along bottom of young plantation. Go through gateway and turn **L** up edge of field. Follow path round behind **Frith Farm Cottages**, down to gate. Turn **L** on road; follow for ½ mile (800m), beside stone wall of **Stalbridge Park**.

❺ At crossroads turn **L**, towards **Frith Farm**. Soon bear **R**, following markers. Path bends **L**, through gate to covered reservoir. Pass and turn **R**, through gate. Descend steps and bear **L** down edge of field (views to manor). Continue on through gap.

❻ When you reach bottom bear **L** into woodland (but not through gate). Walk down ridge, then cross ditch on **L** and continue down edge of field. Go through gateway and retrace your outward route to **church** and your car.

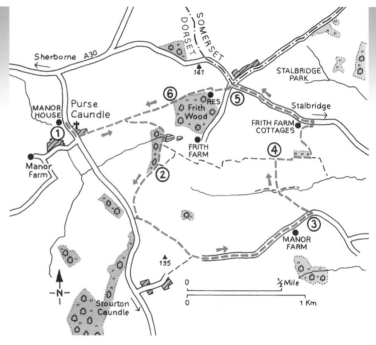

Sherborne Raleigh's Country Retreat

6½ miles (10.4km) 3hrs **Ascent:** 443ft (135m)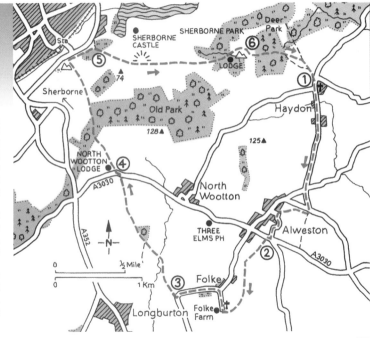

Paths: Country lanes, green lane, field paths, estate tracks, 9 stiles

Suggested map: OS Explorer 129 Yeovil & Sherborne

Grid reference: ST 670157

Parking: On road by church, Haydon village, 2 miles (3.2km) southeast of Sherborne

Around Sherborne, former home of a pirate, politician and poet, Sir Walter Raleigh.

❶ With **church** on L, walk along road and out of **Haydon**. At junction continue ahead ('Bishop's Caundle'). At minor junction cross stile, ahead. Turn **R**, up field edge, towards **Alweston**. Cross stile; bear diagonally **L** over field. Cross stile in corner, go down path; proceed on road, which curves to meet **A3030**.

❷ Turn **R**; turn **L** over stile in hedge. Cross field to gap. Bear diagonally **R** over next field. Halfway along far side go through hedge via stile at corner (yellow marker). Keep ahead along hedge, crossing stiles and footbridges. Continue by wall towards **Folke church**. Cross 2 stiles, go through gate and turn **R** up lane into village, passing church entrance and raised pavement on R. Keep **L** at junction; follow lane round to **L**.

❸ Follow road as it bends sharply **L**; turn **R** up signed bridleway. Follow for 1 mile (1.6km), ascending. It becomes broader and muddier, reaching

main road via gate.

❹ Turn **L** then **R** through gate directly beside **lodge**, up lane. Continue down through woods, with park wall to R. Where drive sweeps R by cottage, keep straight on, up track, passing sports fields on L. Go through 2 gates, cross road and through another gate by lodge on to tarmac track. Follow down steep gorge to main road. Take path immediately **R**, through gate; walk up hill above castle gateway.

❺ Pass through gate into **Sherborne Park**. Follow grassy track ahead, downhill. Go through kissing gate and ahead on estate track (superb views of **castle**). Go up track to thatched lodge, then go through wooden gate and up hill.

❻ At top keep **R**, through gate into woods. Follow track round. Proceed on to tarmac path; pass huge barn on L. Follow track **R**; keep ahead at junction. Descend to lodge; go through gate and straight on to return to car.

Dorset • Southwest England

Cerne Abbas Giant Steps

5½ miles (8.8km) 2hrs 30min **Ascent:** 591ft (180m)

Paths: Country paths and tracks, minor road, main road, 2 stiles

Suggested map: OS Explorer 117 Cerne Abbas & Bere Regis

Grid reference: ST 659043

Parking: Car park (free) opposite church in Minterne Magna

A valley walk from Minterne Magna to see a famous chalk hill carving.

❶ Turn **R** and walk up road through village. Where it curls **L**, turn **R** through gate on to bridleway and go up hill. At top go through gate and bear **L**. Follow blue marker diagonally up to **R**. Go through gate, walk on past trees, then bend up, round field towards trees.

❷ Go through gap and take track down diagonally **L** through woods. At bottom turn **L** along road. After bend take footpath **R**, across field. After trees veer **L**, towards white gate. Cross road, pass **R** of gate, and continue down field. Pass another white gate then continue ahead on road. At end bear **R** on to **A352**.

❸ Cross to car park for best view of **Giant hill carving**. Take road down to village; turn **L** signposted 'Pottery'. Turn **R** by stream ('Village Centre'). Continue over slab bridge and pass old mill. Bear **L**, to high street. Turn **L**, and **L** again in front of **Royal Oak**, to church. Walk up Old Pitch Market to Abbey. Turn **R** into churchyard and bear **L**. Go through gate signposted 'Giant's Hill'; bear **L**.

❹ Cross stile, then turn **R** up steps. Follow path to **L**, round contour of hill, below fence. As path divides, keep **R**, up hill, towards top. Bear **L** along ridge, cross stile by fingerpost and head diagonally **R**, towards barn.

❺ At barn turn **L** and go down through gate. Turn **R** and follow bridleway along hillside with great views towards Minterne Parva. Keep ahead at junction of tracks; dip down through gateway above woods. Keep straight on; go through gate near road. Turn **L** along grassy track. At gateway turn **L** on to gravel lane.

❻ Directly above **Minterne House**, turn **L** through gate and bear **L**. Go through gate and turn **L**, downhill. Continue down through several gates and keep **R** at fingerpost down broad track. Cross stream, then walk up past **church** to return to car park.

Winyard's Gap The Monarch's Way

3¼ miles (5.3km) 1hr 30min **Ascent:** 410ft (125m)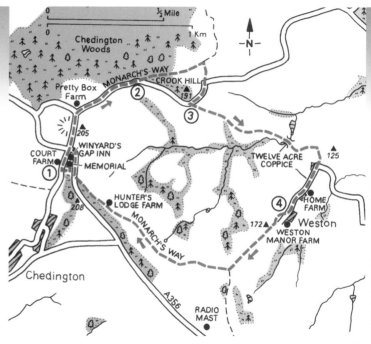

Paths: Field paths, some roads, 1 stile
Suggested map: OS Explorer 117 Cerne Abbas & Bere Regis
Grid reference: ST 491060
Parking: Lay-by north of Chedington, opposite Court Farm

A short walk in Dorset's northern uplands following the route of an historic royal escape.

① Go through gate at back of lay-by; bear **R** on path up through woods. At top of ridge turn **L** for **memorial**. Turn **L** down steps, go back through gate and turn **R** along road. Pass **Winyard's Gap Inn** on R; at junction, cross over and walk up road ahead. Keep **R**, following lane over top of ridge between high banks (**Crook Hill** ahead). After about ½ mile (800m) bear **L** through gate ('**Monarch's Way**').

② Bear **R** along top of field, with **Chedington Woods** falling away on L, and **Crook Hill** ahead and R. Go through gate at foot of hill; bear **R** through woods, round base. Cross stile and bear **L** down field. At farm road near trees, turn **R**. Follow up to lane and turn **R**.

③ Shortly, on corner, go **L** through gate and hook back down fence on bridleway. Go through 2 gates at bottom and continue down field, parallel with top hedge. **Twelve Acre Coppice** (R) is a lovely stretch of mixed woodland. At bottom cross stream via bridge, then go through gate and ahead up track. Go through gate to **L** of barn (blue marker) and turn **R** on farm road, through farmyard. At lane go straight ahead, passing **Home Farm** on L, into **Weston**.

④ Just before **Weston Manor Farm** detour **R** through gate (blue marker). Turn **L** through gate; turn **R** to resume track straight up hill, with radio mast topping ridge ahead. After short tunnel of trees bear **R** through gate along track, part of **Monarch's Way** commemorating Charles II's flight from Cromwell's army. Go through gate and stay on track. Go through another gate with ponds to R. Pass through 2nd gate to **L** of barn, walk past **Hunter's Lodge Farm** and up drive to road. Turn **R** on main road; follow back down to inn, with care. Turn **L** to return to lay-by and your car.

Thorncombe Forde Abbey

5 miles (8km) 2hrs 30min **Ascent:** 443ft (135m)

Paths: Field paths, country lanes, 18 stiles

Suggested map: OS Explorer 116 Lyme Regis & Bridport

Grid reference: ST 373029

Parking: At crossroads south west of Thorncombe

The going is fairly easy through this area renowned for its soft fruit.

❶ Turn **L** (northeast) and walk down into **Thorncombe**. Turn **L** up Chard Street and take footpath on **R** through churchyard. Bear **R** down lane, then **L** on gravel track beside wall, opposite Goose Cottage. Cross stile into field, pass **barn** on L, then go straight on down hedge.

❷ Cross stile in corner; go straight across field. Cross stile and bear diagonally **R**, down to corner of next field. Cross stile, then 2nd stile on **R**. Ford stream and bear **L**, up field. Cross stile on **L**; continue up. Cross another stile on **R**; bear **R** round edge of field. Track veers **R** through hedge. Cross 2 more stiles; continue straight on. By trough turn **L** over pair of stiles; go straight ahead up field edge. Go through gate and bear **R**, towards house.

❸ Emerge through gate on to road; turn **L**. At junction turn **R** on to path; head for woods. Turn **L**

before edge of woods; at corner go **R**, through gate. Head diagonally **L** to bottom corner, opposite **Forde Abbey** gates. Cross stile; turn **R** on road to cross River Axe.

❹ Turn immediately **L** on to footpath; follow past back of **Abbey**. At far corner cross footbridge over river; bear **R** towards lone cedar, then **L** up slope to stile ('**Liberty Trail**'). Cross, then walk along top of woods. Cross stile; bear **L** across fields towards another cedar.

❺ Meet road by **fruit-pickers' camp**. Go across, through gate and up field. Towards top R-H corner bear **R** through gate; keep on this line. Cross pair of stiles in corner, pass **Forde Abbey Farm** on L and keep straight on by hedge. Cross stile and walk down track.

❻ At junction of tracks keep straight on. Where track forks bear L, go through gate and **L** across field. Cross stile in hedge; turn **R** up road. Follow for ½ mile (800m) to return to car.

½ done this one

Seatown Golden Cap in Trust

4 miles (6.4km) 2hrs 30min **Ascent:** 1,007ft (307m) ⚠️

Paths: Field tracks, country lanes, steep zig-zag gravel path, 7 stiles
Suggested map: OS Explorer 116 Lyme Regis & Bridport
Grid reference: SY 420917
Parking: Car park (charge) above gravel beach in Seatown; beware, can flood in stormy weather

Climb a fine cliff top, owned by one of the country's most popular charities, The National Trust.

❶ Walk back up through **Seatown**. Cross stile on **L**, on to footpath ('Coast Path Diversion'). Cross stile at end, bear **L** to cross stile and footbridge into woodland. Cross pair of stiles at other side; bear **R** up hill ('**Golden Cap**').

❷ Where track forks keep **L**. Go through trees and over stile. Bear **L**, straight across open hillside, with National Trust's **Golden Cap** ahead of you. Pass through line of trees and walk up fence. Go up some steps, cross stile and continue ahead. At fingerpost go **L** through gate; follow path of shallow steps up through bracken, heather, bilberry and bramble to top of **Golden Cap**.

❸ Pass trig point and turn **R** along top. Pass stone memorial to Earl of Antrim. At marker stone turn **R** and follow zig-zag path downhill (great views along bay to Charmouth and Lyme Regis). Go through gate and bear **R** over field towards ruined **St Gabriel's Church**. In bottom corner turn down through gate, passing ruins on **R**; go through 2nd gate. Go down track, passing cottages on **L**, and bear **R** up road ('Morcombelake'). Follow up between high banks and hedges. Continue through gateway.

❹ At road junction, turn **R** down **Muddyford Lane** ('**Langdon Hill**'). Pass gate of **Shedbush Farm** and continue straight up hill. Turn **R** up concreted lane towards **Filcombe Farm**. Follow blue markers through farmyard, bearing **L** through 2 gates. Walk up track, go through 2 more gates and bear **L** over top of green saddle between **Langdon Hill** and **Golden Cap**.

❺ Go **L** through gate in corner and down gravel lane (**Pettycrate Lane**) beside woods ('**Seatown**'). Ignore footpath to **R**. At junction of tracks keep **R**, downhill, with patchwork of fields on hillside ahead. Pass **Seahill House** on **L** and turn **R**, on to road. Continue down road into **Seatown** village to return to car.

Great Bedwyn A Working Windmill

5½ miles (8.8km) 2hrs Ascent: 147ft (45m)

Paths: Field paths, woodland tracks, tow path, roads, 1 stile
Suggested map: OS Explorer 157 Marlborough & Savernake Forest
Grid reference: SU 279645
Parking: Great Bedwyn Station

A peaceful canal walk, visiting Wiltshire's only working windmill.

❶ Walk back to main road in **Great Bedwyn** and turn **R**, then **L** down Church Street. Pass **Lloyd's Stone Museum** and church; take footpath **L** between 2 graveyards. Climb stile, cross field to kissing gate; carefully cross railway line to further kissing gate. Cross footbridge, then bridge over **Kennet and Avon Canal** and descend to tow path.

❷ Turn **R**, pass beneath bridge and continue along tow path for 1½ miles (2.4km), passing 3 locks, to Lock 60. Cross canal here, turn **L**, then follow wooded path **R** and through tunnel beneath railway. Ascend steps to **Crofton Pumping Station**.

❸ Retrace steps to tow path and Lock 60. Take footpath **R**, waymarked to **Wilton Windmill**; walk by **Wilton Water** along edge of fields. Eventually, turn **R** down short track to lane by village pond in **Wilton**.

❹ Turn **L**, then just past **Swan Inn**, follow lane **L**

('**Great Bedwyn**'). Climb out of village and fork **R** to pass **Wilton Windmill**. Continue along lane and turn **L** on to track, opposite lane to Marten. Just before wooded track snakes downhill, turn **R** along bridle path (unsigned) beside woodland.

❺ At staggered crossing of paths, turn **R**; in 50yds (46m), turn **L** ('**Great Bedwyn**'). Proceed down well-surfaced track; go through gate into **Bedwyn Brail**. Continue through woods, following signs ('**Great Bedwyn**'). Go straight across clearing before forking **L** to re-enter woods in **L-H** corner of clearing.

❻ On emerging in field corner, keep **L** along field boundary, go through gap in hedge and descend along **L-H** side of next field (**Great Bedwyn** visible ahead). Near bottom of field, bear half **R**, downhill to canal.

❼ Pass through gate by bridge and Lock 64 and turn **R** along tow path. Go through car park to road, then turn **L** over canal and rail bridges before turning **R** back to Great Bedwyn Station.

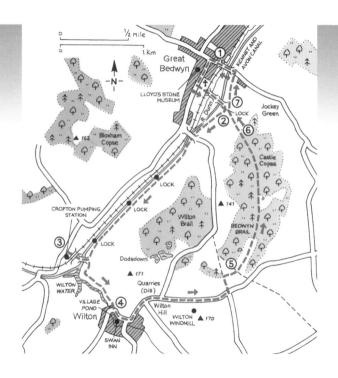

Savernake A Royal Forest

5½ miles (8.8km) 2hrs 30min **Ascent:** 213ft (65m)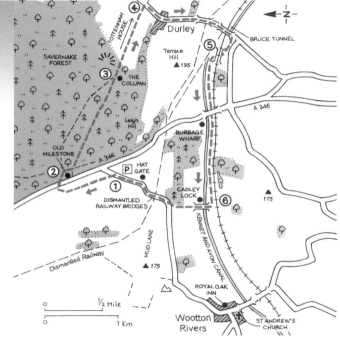

Paths: Woodland tracks, tow path, bridle paths, country lanes
Suggested map: OS Explorer 157 Marlborough & Savernake Forest
Grid reference: SU 215646
Parking: Hat Gate 8 picnic area off A346 south of Marlborough

Through an ancient forest landscape high above Marlborough.

① From car park, turn **R**, then almost immediately **L** past wooden barrier. Follow wooded path for 500yds (457m), then bear **R** to reach **A346**. Cross over near old milestone and take track beyond wooden barrier, signed to **Tottenham House**.

② In 150yds (137m), at major crossing of routes, turn **R** and after similar distance at more minor crossing of paths, turn **L**. Follow this straight track (can be very muddy in places) for ¾ mile (1.2km) to **The Column**, an elegant classical column, built by Thomas Bruce in memory of his uncle, Charles Bruce, former Earl of Ailesbury.

③ Maintain direction towards **Tottenham House**, which is visible in distance. **Savernake Forest** consists of 2,300 acres (931.5ha) of mixed woodland (grand oaks, chestnuts and beeches), managed by Forestry Commission. (Local tradition has it that Henry VIII married Jane Seymour at Savernake, where great barn was hung with tapestries and transformed into banqueting hall for wedding feast.) On leaving woodland, continue along wide fenced track, eventually reaching gate and road opposite drive to **Tottenham House**.

④ Turn **R**, walk through hamlet of **Durley** and keep to lane across old railway bridge, then main railway bridge, and shortly take footpath on **R**, waymarked 'Wootton Rivers'. You are now walking above **Kennet and Avon Canal** as it passes through **Bruce Tunnel**.

⑤ Walk down some steps, pass through narrow and low tunnel under railway line and join canal tow path just below entrance to **Bruce Tunnel**. Turn **L** along tow path for about 1½ miles (2.4km), passing beneath **A346** at **Burbage Wharf** to reach **Cadley Lock**.

⑥ Turn **R** over bridge No 105 and follow metalled track to T-junction. Turn **R** and keep to road, passing 2 dismantled railway bridges, back to car park.

Downton Admiral Lord Nelson

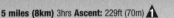

5 miles (8km) 3hrs Ascent: 229ft (70m)

Paths: Riverside paths, downland tracks, metalled lanes, 6 stiles

Suggested map: OS Explorers 130 Salisbury & Stonehenge; 131 Romsey, Andover & Test Valley

Grid reference: SU 180214 (on Explorer 130)

Parking: Plenty of roadside parking in High Street

Discover an 18th-century estate associated with Lord Nelson.

❶ Head west along High Street, cross river bridge and take footpath **R** ('Charlton All Saints'). Walk alongside river, go through kissing gate and keep to footpath as it swings away from river along causeway through water-meadows. Path widens to track; as this bears **L** towards bridge, fork **R** along path to stile and footbridge.

❷ Turn **R** along concrete track; as it bears **L** towards farm buildings, fork **R** across stile and keep to **R-H** field edge to small bridge and stile. Head across field to stile; cross next field to stile by house. Cross drive and stile opposite. Walk beside hedge on **R**, following it **L**; continue ahead to public footbridge.

❸ Cross stile and further footbridge to join footpath through marshland. Pass through gate; cross series of footbridges across weirs and streams to mill. Turn **L** in front of mill and follow driveway. Shortly, take waymarked footpath **L** (bear **R** to chapel), uphill through woodland, eventually reaching fork of paths.

❹ Take main path **R** to stile on woodland edge. Bear half **R** across field to gate (**Trafalgar House**, given to Nelson's heirs in recognition of his services is to R), and follow woodland path for ¼ mile (400m) to metalled lane. Turn **R** uphill and shortly **L** at junction opposite lodge.

❺ Cross bridge over disused railway line and take arrowed bridle path **R**. Do not follow course of old railway, instead keep to **R-H** edge of 2 fields to road.

❻ Turn **R** under bridge; then **L** to follow old embankment. When this ends, maintain direction over hill and descend to cross path.

❼ Descend into valley; as you start climbing, take path to **L** of embankment. Eventually, go through gap in hedge at rear of houses and bear **R** along fenced path. Cross road and continue down path to gate. Walk down drive and turn **L** back to High Street.

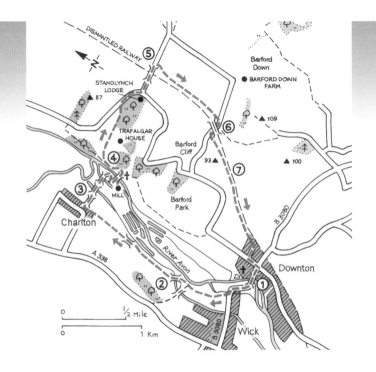

Amesbury Glimpses of Stonehenge

6½ miles (10.4km) 3hrs **Ascent:** 518ft (158m)

Paths: Tracks, field and bridle paths, roads, 3 stiles

Suggested map: OS Explorer 130 Salisbury & Stonehenge

Grid reference: SU 149411

Parking: Free parking at Amesbury Recreation Ground car park

A downland and riverside ramble.

❶ Take footpath to **R** of play area, cross footbridge. Bear **R** to cross main footbridge over **River Avon**. At crossing of tracks, take track ('**Durnford**'); pass **R** of cottages. Head uphill to junction; continue straight on, downhill to gate. Turn **R** along field edge and bear **L** in corner to join path through valley bottom by stream.

❷ Shortly, cross footbridge on **R**; follow path through marshy ground to cross bridge over Avon. Bear **R** over bridge; keep **L** through paddock beside thatched cob wall of **Normanton Down House** to stile. Bear **R** along drive to road. Turn **L** then, in ¼ mile (400m), turn **R** up farm road towards **Springbottom Farm**.

❸ Either walk up tarmac road or join path through spinney on R, latter giving views to Stonehenge. Pass barns and descend to farm. Beyond barns, bear **L** with red byway arrow on to track beside paddocks.

❹ Keep to track through downland valley (Lake Bottom) for ¾ mile (1.2km). Where it becomes metalled at Lake, take arrowed path **R**, up **L-H** edge of field into woodland; bear **L** uphill to stile. Keep **R** along field edge to further stile.

❺ Cross lane and take bridle path **R** in front of thatched house. Head downhill, cross drive and bear **L**; cross 2 footbridges over Avon. Pass beside **Durnford Mill**; follow drive out to lane.

❻ Turn **L** and walk through **Great Durnford**, passing church and drive to **Great Durnford Manor**, following lane **R**, uphill through woodland. Descend and take waymarked bridle path **L** beside house.

❼ Ascend through edge of **Ham Wood**. On leaving wood, bear **R** along path to gate. Keep **R** along edge of 2 fields to gate.

❽ Continue through pastureland; bear **R** across field towards waymarker post at field boundary. Ignore public footpath to R ('Stockport'); walk down field edge to gate to rejoin outward route. Retrace steps into Amesbury.

Pitton Clarendon's Lost Palace

7½ miles (12.1km) 3hrs **Ascent:** 410ft (125m) **2**

Paths: Field paths, woodland tracks, country lanes, 9 stiles

Suggested map: OS Explorer 130 Salisbury & Stonehenge

Grid reference: SU 212312

Parking: Pitton village hall

Exploring ancient woodland for the remains of Clarendon Palace.

1 From car park, cross lane and walk up cul-de sac to **R** of **pub**. In 100yds (91m), take footpath **R**, heading uphill between houses to stile. Proceed across narrow field to stile, then go ahead along **R-H** field edge to stile and gate.

2 Cross track and continue along another track to **R** of woodland. It narrows to path and soon reaches stile and enters **Church Copse**. Where fenced path joins track bear **R** then, at junction on woodland fringe, keep straight on downhill into **Farley** village.

3 At road, turn **R** and pass **All Saints Church** and almshouses. Leave village and, just before 30mph sign, cross stile on **L** and follow hedge **R** to stile to rear of bungalow. Walk down drive, cross lane to gate and follow path through narrow field to stile and gate.

4 Cross footbridge and stile ahead, then proceed across next field (on L of power cables), to stile and

gate. Take track immediately **R** and follow this byway to crossing of tracks. Turn **L** alongside fenced enclosure and, on emerging from wood, head straight across 2 fields and enter further woodland.

5 Walk through woodland alongside clearing to your **R**, and cross lane back into woodland. Leave wood and follow track **R**, then **L** around field edge and soon re-enter wood. Keep ahead where **Clarendon Way** merges from R and continue to ruins of **Clarendon Palace**, which began life as Saxon hunting lodge.

6 From **palace** remains, retrace your steps through wood, keeping **L** along Clarendon Way. Follow path for nearly 1 mile (1.6km) through wood. On emerging, keep straight on down track and cross lane by barn.

7 Pass beside cottages and woodland to your **R**, then walk down fenced path, soon to follow diverted footpath signs to sewage pumping station. At lane turn **L**, then **R**, back to village hall.

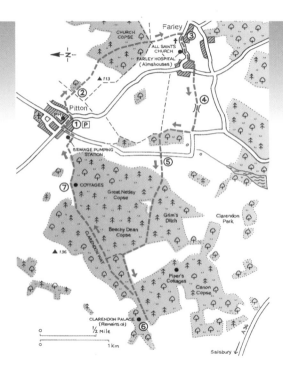

Salisbury A Historic Trail

3 miles (4.8km) 2hrs (longer if visiting attractions) **Ascent:** Negligible

Paths: Pavements and metalled footpaths

Suggested map: OS Explorer 130 Salisbury & Stonehenge; AA Salisbury streetplan

Grid reference: SU 141303

Parking: Central car park (signed off A36 Ring Road)

Around a cathedral city.

1 Join Riverside Walk and follow path through **Maltings Shopping Centre**. Keep by Avon tributary stream to St Thomas Square, close to Michael Snell Tea Rooms and St Thomas' Church. Bear **R** to junction of **Bridge Street**, Silver Street and **High Street**.

2 Turn **L** along Silver Street and cross pedestrian crossing by Haunch of Venison pub to Poultry Cross. Keep ahead along Butcher Row and Fish Row to pass **Guildhall** and **tourist information centre**. Turn **R** along **Queen Street** then **R** along **New Canal**.

3 Return to crossroads; continue along **Milford Street** to pass Red Lion. Turn **R** along **Brown Street**, then **L** along Trinity Street to pass Trinity Hospital. Pass Love Lane into Barnard Street and follow road **R** to St Ann Street, opposite **Joiners' Hall**.

4 Walk down **St Ann Street**; keep ahead on merging with Brown Street to T-junction with St John Street. Cross over and go through **St Ann's Gate** into

Cathedral Close. Pass **Malmesbury House** and Bishops Walk and take path diagonally **L** across green to cathedral's main entrance.

5 Pass entrance, walk beside barrier ahead and turn **R**. Shortly, turn **R** along **West Walk**, passing **Salisbury and South Wiltshire Museum**, Discover Salisbury and **Regimental Museum**. Keep ahead into Chorister Green to pass **Mompesson House**.

6 Bear **L** through gates into **High Street** and turn **L** at crossroads along **Crane Street**. Cross **River Avon** and turn **L** along metalled path beside river through **Queen Elizabeth Gardens**. Keep **L** by play area; soon cross footbridge to follow Town Path across water-meadows to **Old Mill** (hotel) in **Harnham**.

7 Return along Town Path, cross footbridge and keep ahead to **Crane Bridge Road**. Turn **R**, recross **Avon** and turn immediately **L** along riverside path to **Bridge Street**. Cross and follow path ahead towards Bishops Mill. Walk back through **Maltings** to car park.

Wiltshire • Southwest England

3¼ miles (5.3km) 2hrs Ascent: 65ft (20m)
Paths: Field paths (can be muddy), tracks and metalled lanes, 11 stiles
Suggested map: OS Explorer 169 Cirencester & Swindon
Grid reference: SU 101844
Parking: Free parking at Lydiard Country Park

A rural ramble from a Palladian mansion and country park on Swindon's urban fringe.

❶ Turn **L** out of car park, pass **Forest Café** and wooden barrier and continue along track to **Lydiard House**, home of Bolingbroke family who lived here from Elizabethan times (present house built in 1743), and **church**. At **church**, bear **L** through car park, ignoring stile on R, and go through gate. Walk beside walled garden and follow path **L** into woodland.

❷ Just before small clearing, turn **R** (marked by red striped post) to reach kissing gate and cattle grid on woodland edge. Proceed ahead across field on defined path to stile and plank bridge in **R-H** corner.

❸ Continue through edge of small plantation, passing beneath electricity cables, and turn **L** across stile in corner of plantation. Follow waymarker across field to stile and turn **R**, following path within edge of woodland. Bear **L**, then **R**, climb wooden steps and,

emerging in corner of field, turn **L** with red striped post marker and cross stile.

❹ Go across gap (often muddy) between 2 fields to waymarker, then follow **R-H** field edge to stile and gate. Follow farm track ahead; just beyond 1st of 2 metal barriers, turn **R** down track to road.

❺ Turn **R** then, in about 200yds (183m), take arrowed footpath to **L** through gate. Bear half **L** to double stiles and maintain your direction to further stile. Turn sharp **R** along field edge to reach gate by barn, then bear half **L** across field, passing beneath electricity power cables to stile in corner.

❻ Cut diagonally across road to stile and gate. Bear **R** around field edge, alongside small copse to stile. Almost immediately turn **L** through gate and walk down long narrow field. Swing **R** with field boundary and eventually turn **R** across stile by cattle grid encountered on outward route. Retrace steps back to country park and car park.

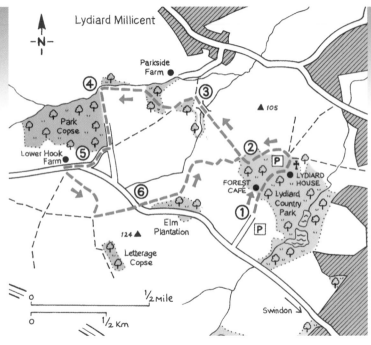

Great Wishford Grovely Wood

5 miles (8km) 2hrs 30min **Ascent:** 370ft (113m)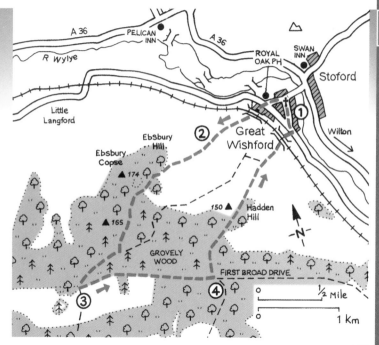

Paths: Woodland paths and downland tracks
Suggested map: OS Explorer 130 Salisbury & Stonehenge
Grid reference: SU 080353
Parking: Roadside parking in South Street, Great Wishford

Learn all about Wiltshire's oldest surviving custom on this peaceful walk through ancient Grovely Wood.

① Return along South Street to **Church** of St Giles and turn **L** at T-junction. Walk past **Royal Oak**. Go under railway bridge and immediately turn **R** along waymarked bridle path beside cemetery. Ascend track to gate.

② Walk along **L-H** field edge to gate, then bear **R** around top of field making for gate that leads into woodland. Turn immediately **L** along woodland track, then turn **L** at next T-junction and walk down well-defined track (permissive bridle path) to another T-junction. Turn **R** up metalled lane.

③ At major junction, turn sharp **L** on to gravel track. Follow it **L**, pass beside metal barrier and join metalled track running down broad beech avenue (**First Broad Drive**) along course of old Roman road, or Lead Road, which traversed Wessex from lead mines of Mendips

in Somerset to join other ancient routes at Old Sarum, such as Harrow Way to Kent. You are now walking through **Grovely Wood**, a fine stretch of woodland that was once used as royal hunting forest and which, together with New Forest and Cranborne Chase, formed very significant preserve.

④ After 1 mile (1.6km), at crossing of public bridle paths, turn **L** and keep to main track downhill through woodland, ignoring all cross paths and forks. Eventually emerge from **Grovely Wood** and follow track downhill towards **Great Wishford**, most southerly of delightful series of villages that nestle in valley of River Wylye. Village is famous for its Oak Apple Day celebrations (29 May), when county's only ancient custom still taking place is enacted by villagers. Pass beneath railway line to lane. Turn **L**, then fork **R** along South Street.

Avebury Pagan Pastures

5 miles (8km) 2hrs 30min **Ascent:** 262ft (80m) ⚠

Paths: Tracks, field paths, some road walking, 3 stiles

Suggested map: OS Explorer 157 Marlborough & Savernake Forest

Grid reference: SU 099696

Parking: Large National Trust car park in Avebury

Explore the famous stone circle and some fine prehistoric monuments.

❶ From car park, walk back to main road and turn **R**. In 50yds (46m), cross and go through gate ('**West Kennett Long Barrow**'). Pass through another gate; follow path alongside **River Kennet**. Go through 2 more gates and cross 2 stiles, your route passing **Silbury Hill**, Europe's largest artificial prehistoric mound.

❷ Beyond gate, walk down **R-H** field edge to gate and **A4**. Cross straight over (carefully) and turn **L**, then almost immediately **R** through gate. Walk down gravel track and cross bridge over stream, track soon narrowing to footpath. Go through kissing gate and turn sharp **L**.

❸ To visit **West Kennett Long Barrow**, 2nd largest barrow in Britain at 300ft (91m) in length, shortly turn **R**. Otherwise go straight on around **L-H** field edge to gate and continue along track. At staggered junction,

keep ahead across stile and walk along **R-H** field boundary. Keep **R** in corner by redundant stile and cross stile on your **R** in next corner and proceed up narrow footpath.

❹ At T-junction, turn **L** and descend to road. Turn **L**, then just beyond bridge, take bridle path sharp **R**. Follow **R-H** field edge to gap in corner and keep **L** through next field. At top you'll see **tumuli** (R) and **The Sanctuary**, site of major wooden buildings, possibly used for religious and burial rites (L). Continue to **A4**.

❺ Cross A4 (care) and head up **Ridgeway**. After 500yds (457m), turn **L** off Ridgeway on to byway. Bear half **R** by clump of trees on **tumuli** and keep to established track, eventually reaching T-junction by series of farm buildings (**Manor Farm**).

❻ Turn **L** ('**Avebury**'), and follow metalled track through earthwork and straight over staggered crossroads by **Red Lion Inn**. Turn **L** opposite National Trust signpost and walk back to car park.

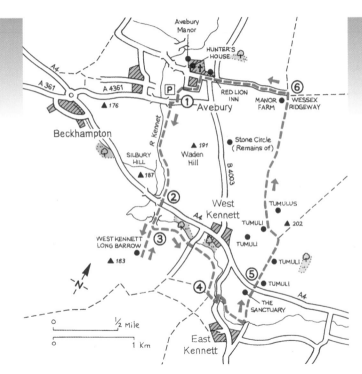

Cricklade The Infant Thames

5½ miles (8.8km) 2hrs 30min **Ascent:** Negligible ⚠

Paths: Field paths and bridle paths, disused railway, town streets, 15 stiles
Suggested map: OS Explorer 169 Cirencester & Swindon
Grid reference: SU 100934
Parking: Cricklade Town Hall car park (free)

An easy ramble across water-meadows.

❶ Turn **R** out of car park, keep ahead at roundabout and walk along High Street. Pass **St Mary's Church** then turn **L** along North Wall before river bridge. Shortly, bear **R** to stile and join Thames Path. Cross stile and continue along field edge to houses.

❷ Go through kissing gate on **R** and bear **L** across field to gate. Follow fenced footpath, cross bridge and pass through gate immediately on **R-H** side. Cross river bridge; turn **L** through gate. Walk beside infant Thames, crossing 2 stiles to enter **North Meadow**.

❸ Cross stile by bridge. Go through gate immediately **R** and keep ahead, ignoring Thames Path **L**. Follow path beside **disused canal**. Cross footbridge and 2 stiles; at fence, bear **R** to cross footbridge close to house ('**The Basin**'). Cross stile and bear **R** along drive.

❹ Cross bridge and turn **L** through gateway. Shortly, bear **R** to join path along **L** side of old canal. Keep to

path for ½ mile (800m) to road. Turn **L** into **Cerney Wick** to T-junction.

❺ Cross stile opposite; keep ahead through paddock to stile and lane. Cross lane and climb stile opposite, continuing ahead to further stile. Shortly, cross stile on **R** and follow path beside lake. Bear **R**, **L** then bear off **L** (yellow arrow) into trees where path becomes track.

❻ Cross footbridge and proceed ahead along field edge to stile. Turn **L** along old railway ('Cricklade'). Cross **Thames** in 1 mile (1.6km) and keep to path along former trackbed to bridge.

❼ Follow gravel path to **Leisure Centre**. Bear **L** on to road, following it **R**; turn **L** opposite entrance to **Leisure Centre** car park. Turn **R**, then next **L** and follow road to church.

❽ Walk beside barrier and turn **L** in front of The Gatehouse into churchyard. Bear **L** to main gates and follow lane to T-junction. Turn **R** to return to car park.

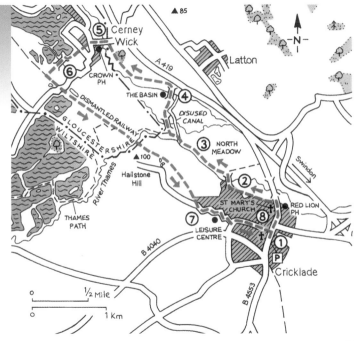

Wardour Old and New Castles

3½ miles (5.7km) 1hr 30min **Ascent:** 278ft (85m)

Paths: Field and woodland paths, parkland tracks, 13 stiles

Suggested map: OS Explorer 118 Shaftesbury & Cranborne Chase

Grid reference: ST 938264

Parking: Free parking at Old Wardour Castle

Rolling parkland around medieval ruins.

❶ From parking area turn **L** along drive and pass between **castle** and **Cresswell's Pond**. Pass Gothic Pavilion then at Wardour House (private) bear **R** with trackway. Gently climb wide track, skirting woodland then at fork keep **L**. At end of woodland, cross stile by field entrance and walk ahead along **R-H** side of field, heading downhill to stile.

❷ Follow path beside **Pale Park Pond** to further stile, then ascend across field to stile and woodland. Shortly, bear **L**, then **R** to join main forest track. Keep **R** at fork and soon leave **Wardour Forest**, passing beside gate on to gravel drive.

❸ At end of drive cross stile on **R**. Head downhill across field to metal gate and follow waymarked path through **Park Copse**, soon to bear **L** down grassy clearing to stile beside field entrance. Follow **R-H** edge towards **Park Gate Farm**.

❹ Cross stile on to farm drive and turn **R** (yellow

arrow) to cross concrete farmyard to gate. Follow path beside hedge to further gate, with River Nadder on **L**, then proceed ahead along **R-H** field edge to stile. Bear diagonally **L** across field, aiming for **L-H** side of cottage. Go through gate and maintain direction to reach stile.

❺ Cross farm drive and stile opposite and head straight uphill, keeping **L** of tree, towards stile and woodland. Follow path **R** through trees and soon bear **L** to pass building on **L**. **New Wardour Castle** is visible on **R**. Keep close to bushes across grounds towards main drive; turn **R** along gravel path and follow sign ('Chapel').

❻ Join drive and walk past **New Wardour Castle**. Where track forks, keep to **R** of stile beside gate. Follow grassy track ahead across parkland towards **Old Wardour Castle**. Climb stile beside gate and proceed ahead, following track uphill to T-junction of tracks. Turn **L**; follow outward route back to car park.

Calne Exploring Bowood Park

7 miles (11.3km) 3hrs 30min Ascent: 360ft (110m)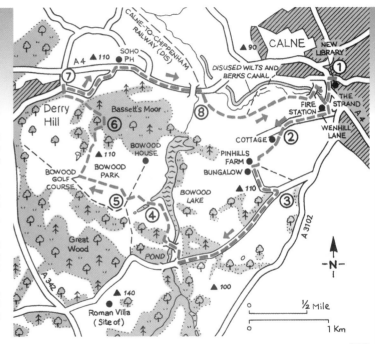

Paths: Field, woodland and parkland paths, metalled drives, pavement beside A4, former railway line, 3 stiles

Suggested map: OS Explorer 156 Chippenham & Bradford-on-Avon

Grid reference: ST 998710

Parking: Choice of car parks in Calne

A visit to one of Wiltshire's grandest houses.

1 Locate **new library** on **The Strand** (**A4**); walk south along New Road to roundabout. Turn **R** along Station Road; take footpath **L** opposite **fire station**. Turn **R** at **Wenhill Lane**; follow it out of built-up area.

2 Near **cottage**, follow waymarker **L** and walk along field edge. Just beyond cottage, climb bank and keep **L** along field edge to bridge and stile. Keep to **L-H** field edge and bear **L** to stile. Follow path **R**, through rough grass around **Pinhills Farm** to stile opposite **bungalow** and turn **L** along drive.

3 At junction, turn **R** along drive; continue for 1 mile (1.6km). Near bridge, take footpath **R**, through kissing gate and walk through parkland beside pond. Cross bridge, go through gate; turn **R** by **Bowood Lake**.

4 Follow path **L** to gate and cross causeway between lakes to gate. Keep straight on up track; follow **L**, then **R** to cross driveway to **Bowood House**.

5 Beyond gate, keep ahead along field edge, then follow path **L** across **Bowood Park**. Keep **L** of trees and field boundary to gate. Turn **R** along drive beside **Bowood Golf Course**. Where drive turns sharp **R** to cottage, keep straight into woodland.

6 Follow path **L**, downhill through clearing (often boggy) along line of telegraph poles. Bear **R** with path back into woodland and follow uphill beside golf course. Turn **R** through break in trees; go through main gates to **Bowood House** into **Derry Hill**.

7 Turn immediately **R** along Old Lane. At **A4**, turn **R** along pavement. Shortly, cross to opposite pavement and continue downhill. Pass beneath footbridge and take drive immediately **R**.

8 Join former **railway** line at Black Dog Halt. Turn **L** and follow back towards **Calne**. Cross disused Canal and turn **R** along tow path. Where path forks keep **R** to Station Road. Retrace steps to town centre.

Bremhill Maud Heath's Causeway

Wiltshire • Southwest England

4 miles (6.4km) 1hr 30min Ascent: 295ft (90m)

Paths: Field paths, bridle paths, metalled roads, 13 stiles

Suggested map: OS Explorer 156 Chippenham & Bradford-on-Avon

Grid reference: ST 980730

Parking: Bremhill church

Follow field paths to a hilltop monument and the start of Maud Heath's Causeway.

1 With your back to **St Martin's Church**, turn **R** and walk downhill through village. Start climbing and take arrowed path **L** across stile. Proceed straight on below bank along field edge to stile in corner. Bear diagonally **R**, uphill across field to gate and lane.

2 Cross stile opposite and paddock to further stile. Bear half-**L** to stile in field corner and walk along **L-H** edge to gate; maintain direction to stile. In next field look out for and pass through gate on your **L** and head across field to gate and lane.

3 Turn **L**, then immediately bear **R** along track to gate. Join waymarked bridle path along **R-H** field edge to gate. Maintain direction through several fields and gates to reach **monument to Maud Heath** on top of **Wick Hill**. It commemorates local widow who, in 1474, made bequest of land and property to provide income to build and maintain causeway from Wick Hill

through Avon marshes to Chippenham.

4 Continue to cross lane via stiles, passing stone tablet and inscription indicating beginning of Maud Heath's Causeway. Follow bridle path along crest of hill through 7 fields via gates and bear **L** before woodland to gate and lane at top of **Bencroft Hill**.

5 Turn **L**, pass **Bencroft Farm** and bungalow, then take waymarked path **R**, through woodland to gate. Continue ahead through plantation, bearing **L** on nearing gate to cross stile. Proceed across field on defined path, cross double fence stiles and remain on path to stile to **L** of bungalow.

6 Turn **L** along lane, heading uphill to junction beside **Dumb Post Inn**. Turn **R**, then **L** along drive to **thatched cottage**. Go through squeeze-stile and keep to **L-H** edge of field through gate and squeeze-stile to reach stile in field corner. Walk in front of **Manor Farm** to reach gate leading into Bremhill churchyard. Bear **R** along path back to car.

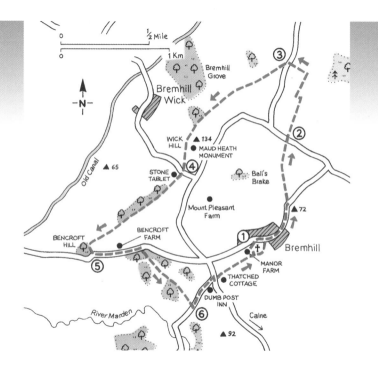

Heytesbury The Chalk Stream

4 miles (6.4km) 2hrs **Ascent:** 49ft (15m)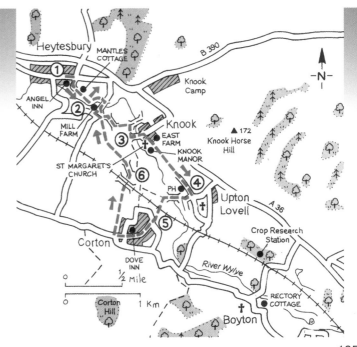
Paths: Field paths and bridleways,10 stiles
Suggested map: OS Explorer 143 Warminster & Trowbridge
Grid reference: ST 926425
Parking: Plenty of room along wide village street

A gentle stroll along the River Wylye.

1 Head east along street, pass **Angel Inn** and turn **R** down Mantles Lane. Where it curves R to become Mill Lane, take footpath **L** along drive beside River Wylye. Bear **R** on to footpath in front of **Mantles Cottage**, go through walk-through stile and walk along **R-H** edge of pasture; soon bear slightly **L** on nearing **Mill Farm** to gate.

2 Beyond further gate, turn **R** across bridge; follow yellow arrow **L** and cross footbridge. Follow Wessex Ridgeway marker ahead at junction then, just before footbridge, turn **L** through gap and bear **R** along field edge. At white wooden arrow, bear half-**L** across field towards thatched cottages to river bank; bear **R** to stile and junction of paths.

3 Turn **L** across footbridge, pass **Knook Manor** and **St Margaret's Church**, then turn **R** by post-box and pass **East Farm** on track (messy after rain). Go through **L-H** of 2 gates and proceed along **R-H** field edge to another gate. Continue into **Upton Lovell**.

4 At crossroads, take signed footpath **R**; just before drive to Hatch House, follow path **L** to footbridge over river. Go through gate and ahead along field edge to metal gate. Cross stile on **L**, walk along hedged path and cross railway (care) via gates and steps. Continue to lane in **Corton**.

5 Turn **L** through village, passing **Dove Inn**. At T-junction, take arrowed path across stile on **R**. Head across field on defined path to stile; keep ahead along fenced path to further stile and proceed along **R-H** edge of field. Shortly, climb stile and turn **L** along field edge to stile and pass beneath railway.

6 Cross footbridge, then stile and walk beside **R-H** fence to gate. From here, follow track ahead. Cross another stile and keep to track until lane. Turn **R**; go through complex of buildings at Mill Farm and across river to rejoin outward route beside River Wylye back into **Heytesbury**.

Fonthill Fantastic Folly

4¼ miles (6.8km) 2hrs **Ascent:** 278ft (85m)

Paths: Tracks, field and woodland paths, parkland, some road walking

Suggested map: OS Explorer 143 Warminster & Trowbridge

Grid reference: ST 933316

Parking: Lay-by close to southern end of Fonthill Lake

Explore Fonthill Park, ridge-top woodlands and pastures around Fonthill Bishop.

❶ With your back to lay-by, turn **R** along road (this can be busy) that traverses **Fonthill Park** beside its beautiful tree-fringed lake for just over ½ mile (800m). Pass beneath magnificent **stone arch** and shortly bear **R** to B3089. Keep to **R** along pavement into pretty little village of **Fonthill Bishop**.

❷ Turn **R** just beyond bus shelter on to track. On passing 'Private Road' sign for Fonthill Estate, turn **L** through small **business park** on unsigned footpath. (William Beckford acquired estate in mid-18th century. His son built Gothic fantasy palace, one of most remarkable buildings in country, in woodland west of lake. It eventually collapsed during a storm.) Keep **L** and soon join track that bears **R** uphill towards woodland. Follow grassy track beside **Fonthill Clump** and keep to main track above valley. In ½ mile (800m) bear **R** downhill into **Little Ridge Wood**.

❸ Track gives way to path. At T-junction, bear **L** and keep **L** at next 2 junctions, following wide path to gate and lane. Turn **R** through hamlet of **Ridge**. Pass **telephone box**, walk uphill and bear off **R** with yellow arrow along drive to **Fonthill House**, which lies above sweeping pastureland.

❹ In ¼ mile (400m), fork **L** with footpath sign to follow track by paddocks to pass beside gate. In 20yds (18m) fork **R** with yellow arrow and walk beside woodland. On entering field, turn **L** along field edge (path becomes defined grassy track around field edge). Gradually descend towards woodland.

❺ Enter wood and bear **L** then **R** along gravel track beside **Fonthill Lake**, which was used as location for filming Joanne Harris's novel *Chocolat*. Cross weir to gate. Disregard track which goes ahead uphill and bear off **R** along lakeside edge. Follow well-established path through 2 gates, eventually returning to parking area.

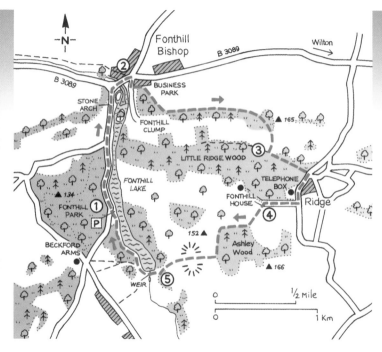

Tollard Royal Around Rushmore Park

4½ miles (7.2km) 2hrs **Ascent:** 616ft (188m) ▲

Paths: Field and woodland paths, bridle paths and tracks

Suggested map: OS Explorer 118 Shaftesbury & Cranborne Chase

Grid reference: ST 944178

Parking: By pond in Tollard Royal

A walk in the heart of Cranborne Chase.

❶ Facing pond turn **L** along track and take waymarked path **R** across footbridge to stile. Follow narrow path half-**L** uphill through scrub and along field edge; soon bear **R** to gate in top corner. Continue, pass to **R** of copse; bear **L** through gates into adjacent field. Keep to **R**-**H** edge, downhill to gate and stile.

❷ Bear diagonally **L** and descend to gate and junction of paths in valley bottom. Take track **R**, through gate and continue to fork of tracks. Ascend track ahead and follow it beside woodland for ½ mile (800m). Bear **R** through trees to metalled lane.

❸ Turn **R**, then **L** before gates to **Rushmore Park**. Keep to established track, heading downhill to crossing of paths by **golf course**.

❹ Turn **R**, pass in front of cottage and keep to path through rough grass alongside fairway. Bear **R** on to track and follow it **L** to reach redundant gateposts. Pass beside gate posts and follow track **R**. Where this peters out, keep ahead beside woodland, bearing **R** to pass green on **L**.

❺ Bear **R** through gate into woodland and follow yellow waymarker **R** through trees. Ill-defined at first, path soon bears **L** to become clear route (yellow arrows) through **Brookes Coppice**, to reach T-junction with track.

❻ Turn **L**, cross drive and stile opposite and bear half-**R** across parkland to stile beyond avenue of trees. Bear slightly **L** downhill to gate in field corner. Shortly take 2nd arrowed path sharp **R**.

❼ Follow track through **Tinkley Bottom** to gate and pass below **Rushmore Farm**. On passing through 2nd of 2 gateways, turn immediately **L** and walk uphill to pair of gates. Go through **L**-**H** gate; keep **R** through 2 paddocks to reach gate.

❽ Take path ahead and bear diagonally **R** downhill to gate and **B3081**. Keep ahead into **Tollard Royal** back to pond and your car.

97 Castle Combe A Picture-book Village

5¾ miles (9.2km) 2hrs 30min **Ascent:** 515ft (157m)

Paths: Field and woodland paths and tracks, metalled lanes, 10 stiles

Suggested map: OS Explorer 156 Chippenham & Bradford-on-Avon

Grid reference: ST 845776

Parking: Free car park just off B4039 at Upper Castle Combe

Through the hilly and wooded By Brook Valley from a famous Wiltshire village.

❶ Leave car park via steps and turn **R**. At T-junction, turn **R**; follow lane into Castle Combe. Keep **L** at **Market Cross**, cross By Brook and continue along road to take path ('Long Dean'), across 2nd bridge on **L**.

❷ Cross stile and follow path uphill then beside **R-H** fence above valley (**Macmillan Way**). Beyond open area, ascend through woodland to stile and gate. Cross further stile; descend into **Long Dean**.

❸ Pass **mill** and follow track **R** to cross river bridge. At **mill house**, keep **R** and follow sunken bridleway uphill to gate. Shortly enter pasture and follow path around top edge, bearing **L** to stile and lane.

❹ Turn **L** and descend to **A420** at **Ford**. Turn **R** along pavement and **R** again into **Park Lane**. (To visit **White Hart** in **Ford**, take road ahead on **L**, 'Colerne'.) Climb gravel track and take footpath **L** through squeeze stile.

❺ Keep **R** through pasture and continue through trees to water-meadow in valley bottom. Turn **L**, cross stream and ascend grassy slope ahead, bearing **L** beyond trees towards waymarker post. Follow footpath along top of field to stile and gate, then walk through woodland to gate and road.

❻ Turn **L**, then immediately **L** again ('North Wraxall'). Keep to road for ¼ mile (400m) and take arrowed bridleway **R**. Follow track then, just before gate, keep **R** downhill on sunken path to footbridge over **Broadmead Brook**.

❼ Shortly, climb stile on **R** and follow footpath close to river. Cross stile and soon pass beside **Nettleton Mill House**, bearing **R** to hidden gate. Walk beside stream and cross stile to **golf course**.

❽ Turn **R** along track, cross bridge. Turn **R**. At gate, follow path **L** below **golf course**. Follow wall to stile on **R**. Descend steps to drive and keep ahead to **Castle Combe**. Turn **L** at **Market Cross** and retrace steps.

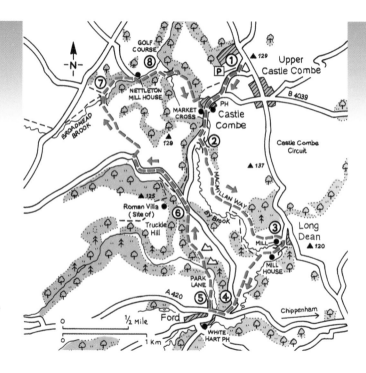

Lacock Birthplace of Photography

2 miles (3.2km) 1hr **Ascent:** 16ft (5m)

Paths: Field paths and tracks; some road walking, 6 stiles

Suggested map: OS Explorer 156 Chippenham & Bradford-on-Avon

Grid reference: ST 918681

Parking: Free car park on edge of Lacock

A stroll around England's finest medieval village with a riverside walk and a visit to Lacock Abbey.

❶ From car park entrance, cross road and follow gravel path into village, passing entrance to **Lacock Abbey** and **Fox Talbot Museum**, housed in beautifully restored 16th-century barn, commemorating William Henry Fox Talbot, pioneer of photography. Abbey began as Augustinian nunnery and was eventually sold to Talbot family. Turn **R** into **East Street** opposite **Red Lion** and walk down to Church Street. Turn **L**, pass timber-framed Sign of the Angel Inn with its medieval layout and magnificent 16th-century doorway and bear **L** into **West Street** opposite George Inn, which dates back to 1361. Shortly, follow road **L** into High Street.

❷ Pass National Trust shop and turn **L** to walk back down along East Street. Turn **R** on Church Street and bear **L** in front of **St Cyriac's Church** with its fine

wagon roof and grandiose Renaissance tomb of Sir William Sharrington, to reach ancient packhorse bridge beside ford across Bide Brook. Follow path beside stream then continue up lane beside cottages to end of road.

❸ Go through kissing gate on your **R** and follow tarmac path across field to gate and pass stone cottages at **Reybridge** to lane. Turn **R** along lane, then **R** again to cross bridge over **River Avon**.

❹ Immediately cross stile on your **R** and bear diagonally **L** to far corner where you rejoin river bank to reach stile. Walk beside river for 300yds (274m) to further stile and cross field following line of telegraph poles to stile. Keep straight on to stile beside gate then head towards stone bridge over Avon.

❺ Climb stile and turn **R** across bridge. Join raised pavement and follow this back into village and car park.

Corsham A Wealthy Weaving Town

4 miles (6.4km) 2hrs **Ascent:** 114ft (35m)

Paths: Field paths and country lanes, 10 stiles

Suggested map: OS Explorer 156 Chippenham & Bradford-on-Avon

Grid reference: ST 871704

Parking: Long stay car park in Newlands Lane

Explore this unexpected architectural town and adjacent Corsham Park.

❶ Turn **L** out of car park, then **L** again along Post Office Lane to High Street. Turn **L**, pass **tourist information centre** and turn **R** into Church Street. Pass impressive entrance to **Corsham Court** and enter **St Bartholomew's churchyard**.

❷ Follow path **L** to gate; walk ahead to join main path across **Corsham Park**. Turn **L**; walk along south side of park, passing **Corsham Lake**, to stile and gate. Keep ahead on fenced path beside track to kissing gate and proceed across field to stile and lane.

❸ Turn **L**, pass **Park Farm**, splendid stone farmhouse on **L**, and shortly take waymarked footpath **R** along drive to pass **Rose and Unicorn House**. Cross stile and follow **R-H** field edge to stile, then bear half-**L** to stone stile in field corner. Ignore path arrowed **R** and head straight across field to further stile and lane.

❹ Take footpath opposite, bearing half-**L** to stone stile to L of **cottage**. Maintain direction and pass through field entrance to follow path along **L-H** side of field to stile in corner. Turn **L** along road for ½ mile (800m) to **A4**.

❺ Go through gate in wall on **L** and follow worn path **R**, across centre of parkland pasture to metal kissing gate. Proceed ahead to reach kissing gate on edge of woodland. Follow wide path to further gate and bear half-**R** to stile.

❻ Keep ahead on worn path across field and along field edge to gate. Continue to further gate with fine views R to **Corsham Court**. Follow path **R** along field edge, then where it curves R, bear **L** to join path beside churchyard wall to stile.

❼ Turn **L** down avenue of trees to gate and town centre (**almshouses** on L). Turn **R** along Pickwick Road, then **R** again along pedestrianised High Street. Turn **L** back along Post Office Lane to car park.

Bradford-on-Avon A Miniature Bath

3½ miles (5.7km) 1hr 45min **Ascent:** 164ft (50m) ⚠

Paths: Tow path, field and woodland paths, metalled lanes

Suggested map: OS Explorers 142 Shepton Mallet;156 Chippenham & Bradford-on-Avon

Grid reference: ST 824606 (on Explorer 156)

Parking: Bradford-on-Avon Station car park (charge)

Combine a visit to this enchanting riverside town with a canal-side stroll.

❶ Walk to end of car park, away from station, and follow path **L** beneath railway and beside River Avon. Enter **Barton Farm Country Park** and keep to path across grassy area to information board. Here you can visit craft shops in former medieval farm buildings and marvel at great beams and rafters of Bradford-on-Avon's magnificent tithe barn, 2nd largest in Britain. With packhorse bridge R, keep ahead to **R** of **tithe barn** to **Kennet and Avon Canal**.

❷ Turn **R** along tow path. Cross bridge over canal in ½ mile (800m) and follow path **R** to footbridge and stile. Proceed along **R-H** field edge to further stile, then bear diagonally **L** uphill away from canal to kissing gate.

❸ Follow path through edge of woodland. Keep to path as it bears **L** uphill through trees to reach metalled lane. Turn **R** and walk steeply downhill to **Avoncliff** and **canal**.

❹ Don't cross aqueduct, instead pass Mad Hatter Tea Rooms, descend steps on your **R** and pass beneath canal. Keep **R** by **Cross Guns** and join tow path towards Bradford-on-Avon. Continue for ¾ mile (1.2km) to bridge passed on your outward route.

❺ Bear off **L** downhill along metalled track and follow it beside River Avon back into **Barton Farm Country Park**. Cross packhorse bridge and railway to Barton Orchard.

❻ Follow alleyway to Church Street and continue ahead to pass **Holy Trinity Church** and **Saxon Church of St Laurence**, jewel in Bradford-on-Avon's crown and not to be missed. Founded by St Aldhelm, Abbot of Malmesbury in AD 700, this building dates back to 10th century. Cross footbridge and walk through St Margaret's car park to road. Turn **R**, then **R** again back into station car park.

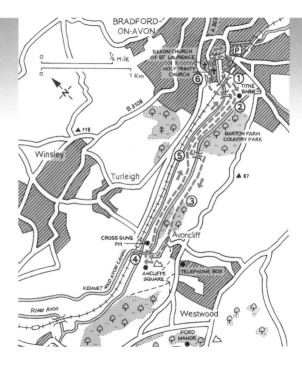

Walking in Safety

All these walks are suitable for any reasonably fit person, but less experienced walkers should try the easier walks first. Route finding is usually straightforward, but you will find that an Ordnance Survey map is a useful addition to the route maps and descriptions.

Risks

Although each walk here has been researched with a view to minimising the risks to the walkers who follow its route, no walk in the countryside can be considered to be completely free from risk. Walking in the outdoors will always require a degree of common sense and judgement to ensure that it is as safe as possible.

- Be particularly careful on cliff paths and in upland terrain, where the consequences of a slip can be very serious. Check tidal conditions before walking on the seashore.

- Some sections of route are by, or cross, busy roads. Take care and remember traffic is a danger even on minor country lanes.

- Be careful around farmyard machinery and livestock, especially if you have children or a dog with you.

- Be aware of the consequences of changes in the weather and check the forecast before you set out. Carry spare clothing and a torch if you are walking in the winter months. Remember the weather can change very quickly at any time of the year, and in moorland and heathland areas, mist and fog can make route finding much harder. Don't set out in these conditions unless you are confident of your navigation skills in poor visibility. In summer remember to take account of the heat and sun; wear a hat and carry spare water for you and your dog.

- On walks away from centres of population you should carry a whistle and survival bag. If you do have an accident requiring the emergency services, make a note of your position as accurately as possible and dial 999.